# SONGS OF THE
# 1970s

 96 Songs with Online Audio Backing Tracks

D1591959

To access audio visit:
**www.halleonard.com/mylibrary**

Enter Code
6499-4031-6107-4276

ISBN 978-1-4950-0034-8

HAL•LEONARD®
CORPORATION

7777 W. BLUEMOUND RD. P.O. BOX 13819 MILWAUKEE, WI 53213

Visit Hal Leonard Online at
**www.halleonard.com**

# ABC

Words and Music by ALPHONSO MIZELL,
FREDERICK PERREN, DEKE RICHARDS and BERRY GORDY

**With drive**

Buh, buh, buh, buh, buh, boo, buh, buh, buh, buh, buh, buh. You

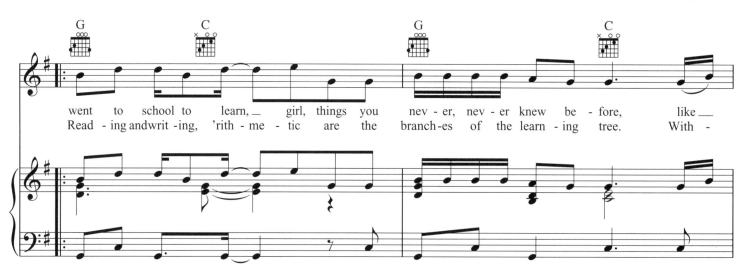

went to school to learn,__ girl, things you nev - er, nev - er knew be - fore, like__
Read - ing and writ - ing, 'rith - me - tic are the branch - es of the learn - ing tree. With -

"I" be - fore "E" ex - cept af - ter "C" and why two plus two makes four. Now, now, now__
out the roots of a love ev - 'ry day, girl, your ed - u - ca - tion ain't com - plete.

To Coda

# AFTERNOON DELIGHT

Words and Music by
BILL DANOFF

In a moderately slow Country 2

Gon - na find my ba - by, gon - na hold her tight, gon - na grab some af - ter - noon _____ de - light. _____ My mot - to's al - ways been "When it's right, it's right." Why wait un - til the mid - dle of a cold, dark night

10

# AIN'T NO SUNSHINE

Words and Music by
BILL WITHERS

(drums)

# AMERICAN PIE

Words and Music by
DON McLEAN

A long, long time a- go I can still re- mem- ber how that

mu- sic used to make me smile. _____ And

I knew if I had my chance that I could make those peo- ple dance and

17

*Additional Lyrics*

2. Now for ten years we've been on our own,
   And moss grows fat on a rollin' stone
   But that's not how it used to be
   When the jester sang for the king and queen
   In a coat he borrowed from James Dean
   And a voice that came from you and me
   Oh and while the king was looking down,
   The jester stole his thorny crown
   The courtroom was adjourned,
   No verdict was returned
   And while Lenin read a book on Marx
   The quartet practiced in the park
   And we sang dirges in the dark
   The day the music died
   We were singin'...bye-bye...etc.

3. Helter-skelter in the summer swelter
   The birds flew off with a fallout shelter
   Eight miles high and fallin' fast,
   It landed foul on the grass
   The players tried for a forward pass,
   With the jester on the sidelines in a cast
   Now the half-time air was sweet perfume
   While the sergeants played a marching tune
   We all got up to dance
   But we never got the chance
   'Cause the players tried to take the field,
   The marching band refused to yield
   Do you recall what was revealed
   The day the music died
   We started singin'... bye-bye...etc.

4. And there we were all in one place,
   A generation lost in space
   With no time left to start again
   So come on, Jack be nimble, Jack be quick,
   Jack Flash sat on a candlestick
   'Cause fire is the devil's only friend
   And as I watched him on the stage
   My hands were clenched in fits of rage
   No angel born in hell
   Could break that Satan's spell
   And as the flames climbed high into the night
   To light the sacrificial rite
   I saw Satan laughing with delight
   The day the music died
   He was singin'...bye-bye...etc.

# AT SEVENTEEN

Words and Music by
JANIS IAN

# BABY BLUE

Words and Music by
PETER HAM

To Coda ⊕ B♭

my ba - by blue. ____
my ba - by blue. ____
my Dix - ie dear. __

1.

2.

Dm   Gm   D+/F♯

What can I do, ____ what can I say? _
How can I show ____ you? ____ Show me the way. _

Cm   Cm/B♭   A♭

____
____
Ex - cept that I want _
Don't you ____ know _

# BABY COME BACK

Words and Music by JOHN C. CROWLEY
and PETER BECKETT

# BAD, BAD LEROY BROWN

Words and Music by
JIM CROCE

# BLACK DOG

Words and Music by JIMMY PAGE,
ROBERT PLANT and JOHN PAUL JONES

Hey hey, ba - by, when you walk that way, _ watch your hon - ey drip; _ can't keep a - way. _

50

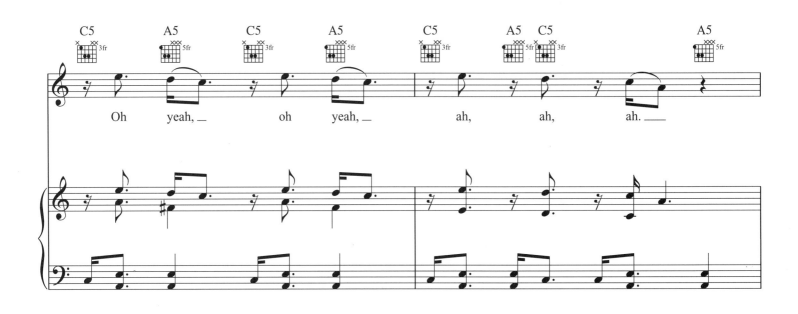

Oh yeah, __ oh yeah, __ ah, ah, ah. ___

2025-06-09

# CANDLE IN THE WIND

Words and Music by ELTON JOHN
and BERNIE TAUPIN

**Gently, reflectively**

Good-bye, Nor - ma Jean, _____ though I nev - er knew you _____ at all
Lone - li - ness _____ was tough, _____ the tough - est role you ev - er played.

you had the grace to hold your - self _____ while those a - round _____ you crawled. _____
Hol - ly - wood cre - at - ed a su - per - star _____ and pain was the price you paid. _____

They crawled out of the wood - work
E - ven when you died,

# BRIDGE OVER TROUBLED WATER

Words and Music by
PAUL SIMON

**Moderately, like a Spiritual**

When you're wea - ry, ___ feel - in' ___

down and out, ___ when you're on the

___ small, when tears are in your eyes, _

street, when eve - ning falls so hard, _

Sail on, sil - ver girl,      sail on

64

# CAT'S IN THE CRADLE

Words and Music by HARRY CHAPIN
and SANDY CHAPIN

72

# COPACABANA
## (At the Copa)

Music by BARRY MANILOW
Lyric by BRUCE SUSSMAN and JACK FELDMAN

Moderately, with a Latin feel

Her name was Lo - la; ___ she was a
Ri - co; ___ he wore a
Lo - la; ___ she was a

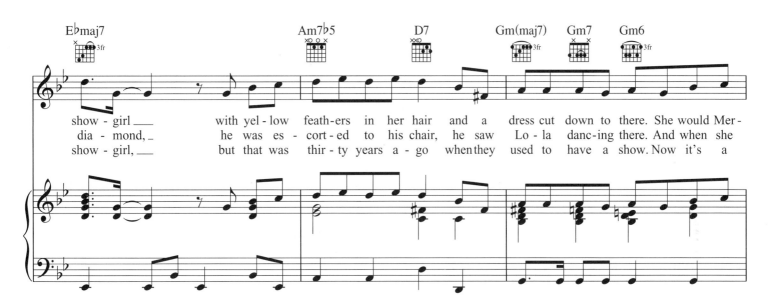

show - girl ___ with yel - low feath - ers in her hair and a dress cut down to there. She would Mer -
dia - mond, _ he was es - cort - ed to his chair, he saw Lo - la danc - ing there. And when she
show - girl, ___ but that was thir - ty years a - go when they used to have a show. Now it's a

74

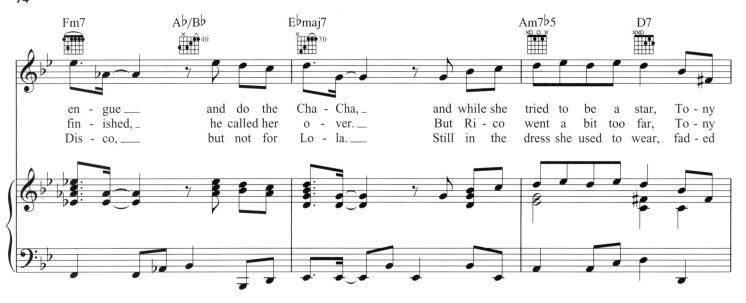

en - gue ___ and do the Cha - Cha, ___ and while she tried to be a star, To - ny
fin - ished, ___ he called her o - ver. ___ But Ri - co went a bit too far, To - ny
Dis - co, ___ but not for Lo - la. ___ Still in the dress she used to wear, fad - ed

al - ways tend - ed bar, a - cross the crowd - ed ___ floor. They worked from
sailed a - cross the bar. And then the punch - es ___ flew and chairs were
feath - ers in her hair, she sits there so re - fined and drinks her-

eight to ___ four. They were young and they had each oth - er, who could
smashed in ___ two. There was young blood and a sin - gle gun - shot, but just
self half ___ blind. She lost her youth and she lost her To - ny, now she's

# (They Long to Be)
# CLOSE TO YOU

Lyric by HAL DAVID
Music by BURT BACHARACH

# CRACKLIN' ROSIE

Words and Music by
NEIL DIAMOND

# Dancing Queen

Words and Music by BENNY ANDERSSON,
BJÖRN ULVAEUS and STIG ANDERSON

# DANIEL

Words and Music by ELTON JOHN
and BERNIE TAUPIN

**Moderately fast**

Dan - iel is trav -
They say Spain is pret -
*Instrumental*

- 'ling to - night ___ on a plane. ___
- ty, ___ though I've nev - er been. ___

Oh God, _____ it looks like Dan - iel.

Must be _____ the clouds _____ in _____ my eyes. _____

# FREE BIRD

Words and Music by ALLEN COLLINS
and RONNIE VAN ZANT

**Slowly**

Lyrics:
If I leave __ here to-mor-row,
Bye, bye, ba-by, it's been a sweet love,

would you still re-mem-ber
though this feel-ing I can't

me?
change.

For I must be __ trav-'ling on now,
But please don't take __ it so bad-ly,

# DECEMBER 1963
## (Oh, What a Night)

Words and Music by ROBERT GAUDIO
and JUDY PARKER

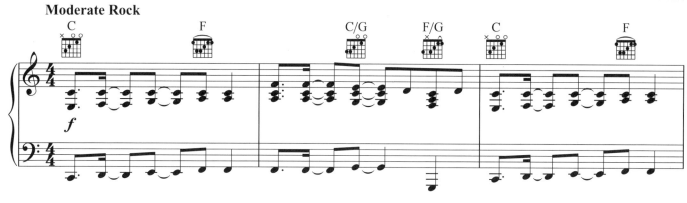

Oh, what a night,
night.

*Instrumental solo*

late De - cem - ber back in
You know, I did - n't e - ven
Hyp - no - tiz - in', mez - mer -
Why'd it take __ so long to

six - ty - three. __ What a ver - y spe - cial time for me, __ as
know her __ name, __ but I was nev - er gon - na be the same. __
iz - ing __ me, __ she was ev - 'ry - thing I dreamed she'd be. __
see the __ light? __ Seemed so wrong, _ but now it seems so right. _

* End, using added cues, 2nd time

# DREAM ON

Words and Music by
STEVEN TYLER

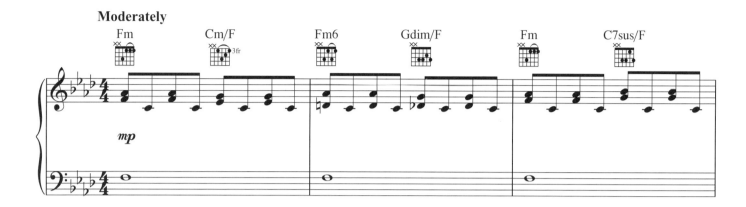

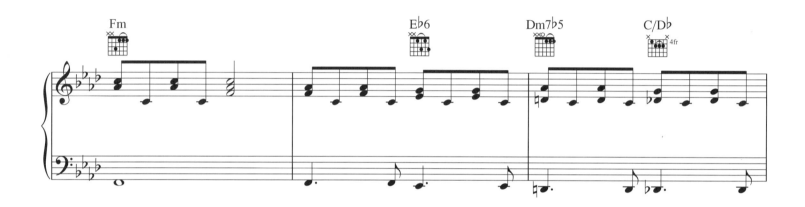

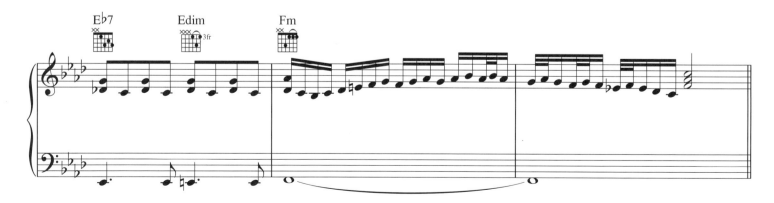

114

# DUST IN THE WIND

Words and Music by
KERRY LIVGREN

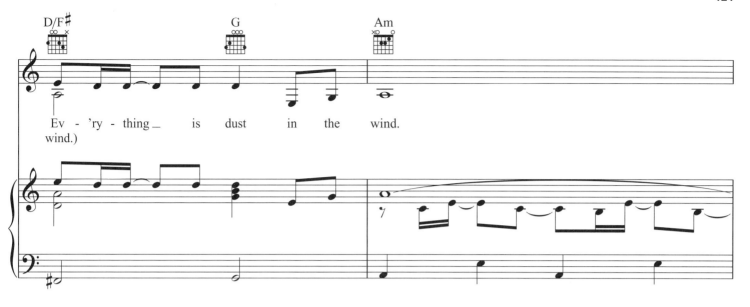

Ev - 'ry - thing __ is dust in the wind.
wind.)

**Repeat and Fade**

**Optional Ending**

*poco rit.*

# EASY

Words and Music by
LIONEL RICHIE

Know it sounds fun-ny, but I just can't stand the pain.

Girl, I'm leav-ing you to-mor-row.

Seems to me, girl, you know I've done all I can.

You see, I begged, stole ___ and I bor - rowed. ___ Yeah, ___

ooh. That's why I'm eas - y, ___ (Ah) ___

I'm eas-y like Sun-day morn - ing. (Ah) ___

That's why I'm eas - y. ___

# EVERYTHING IS BEAUTIFUL

Words and Music by
RAY STEVENS

Moderately fast

Je - sus loves the lit - tle chil - dren, all the lit - tle chil - dren of the world. Red and yel - low, black and white, they are pre - cious in His sight, Je - sus loves the lit - tle chil - dren of the world. _____ Ev - 'ry - thing is

131

*Additional Lyrics*

2. We shouldn't care about the length of his hair or the color of his skin,
   Don't worry about what shows from without but the love that lies within.
   We gonna get it all together now and everything gonna work out fine,
   Just take a little time to look on the good side, my friend, and straighten it out in your mind.

# The First Time Ever I Saw Your Face

Words and Music by
EWAN MacCOLL

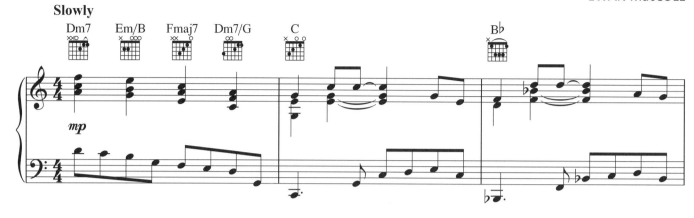

The first __ time _____
The first __ time _____
The first __ time _____

ev-er I saw your face, _____
ev-er I kissed your mouth, _____
ev-er I lay with you _____

the dark _____ and the end of the skies.
was there _____ at my com -

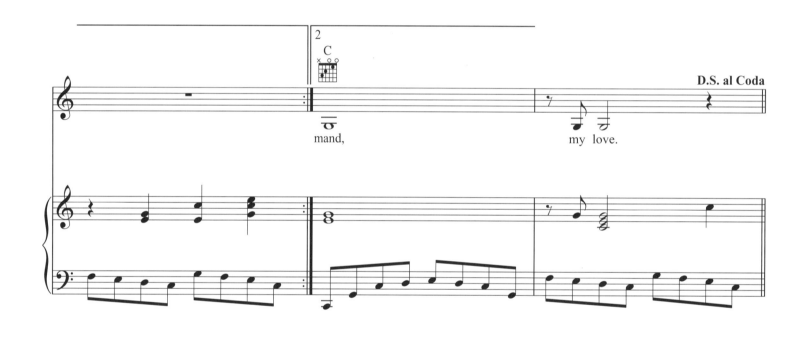

D.S. al Coda

mand, my love.

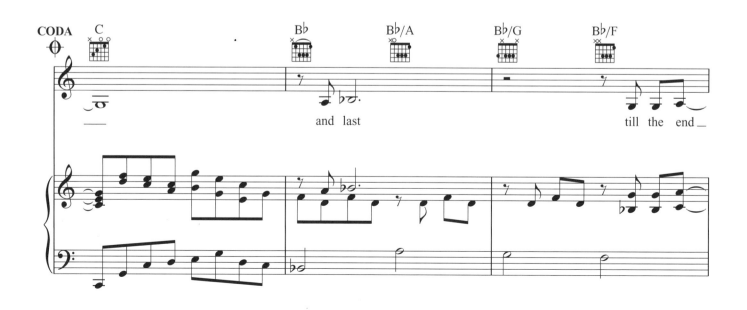

and last till the end __

# GARDEN PARTY

Words and Music by
RICK NELSON

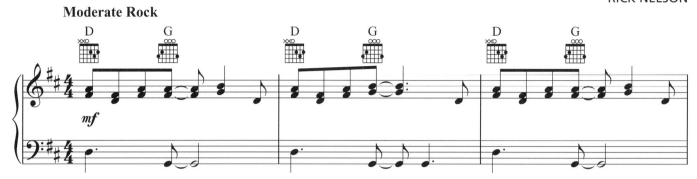

**Moderate Rock**

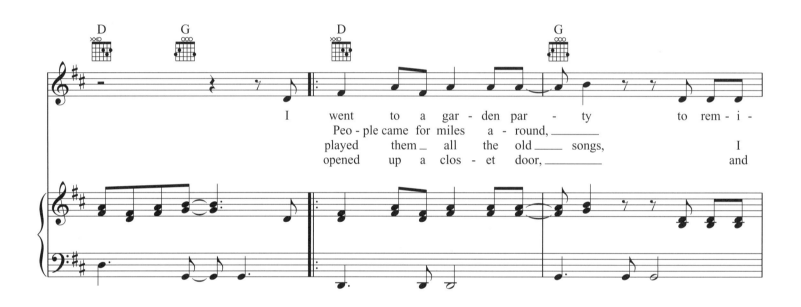

I went to a gar - den par - ty to rem - i -
Peo - ple came for miles a - round, _____
played them ___ all the old ___ songs, _____ I
opened up a clos - et door, _____ and

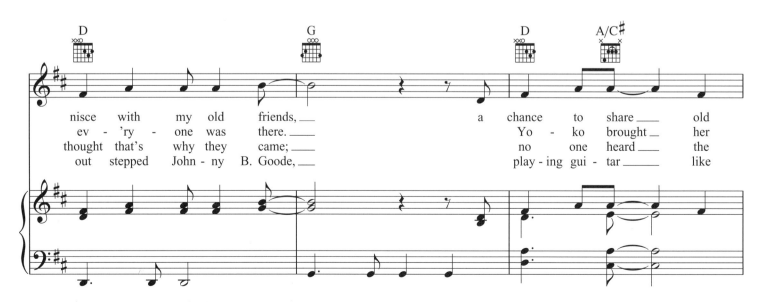

nise with my old friends, ___ a chance to share ___ old
ev - 'ry - one was there. ___ Yo - ko brought ___ her
thought that's why they came; ___ no one heard ___ the
out stepped John - ny B. Goode, ___ play - ing gui - tar ___ like

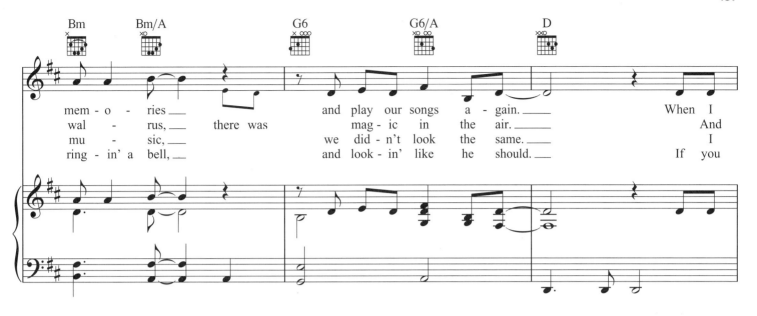

mem - o - ries ___ and play our songs a - gain. ___ When I
wal - rus, ___ there was mag - ic in the air. ___ And
mu - sic, ___ we did - n't look the same. ___ I
ring - in' a bell, ___ and look - in' like he should. ___ If you

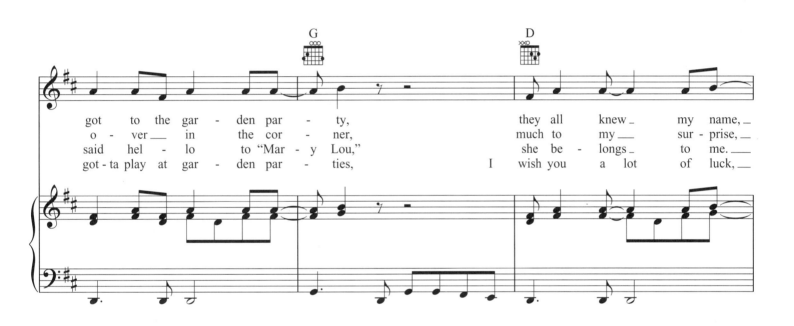

got to the gar - den par - ty, they all knew ___ my name, ___
o - ver ___ in the cor - ner, much to my ___ sur - prise, ___
said hel - lo to "Mar - y Lou," she be - longs ___ to me. ___
got - ta play at gar - den par - ties, I wish you a lot of luck, ___

___ but no one rec - og - nized ___ me,
___ Mis - ter Hughes ___ hid in Dy - lan's shoes,
___ When I sang a song ___ 'bout a hon - ky - tonk,
___ but if mem - o - ries ___ were all ___ I sang,

# HEART OF GLASS

Words and Music by DEBORAH HARRY
and CHRIS STEIN

peace of mind, yet I fear I'm los - ing you. It's

just no good, you teas - ing like you do.

could-'ve made it cruis - ing, yeah. _____

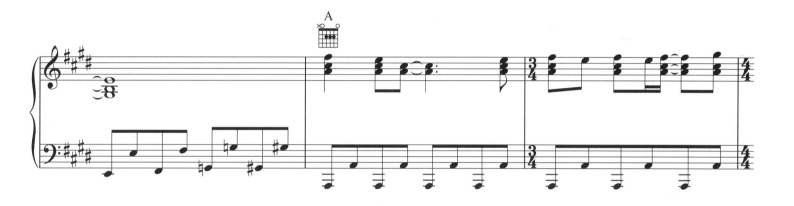

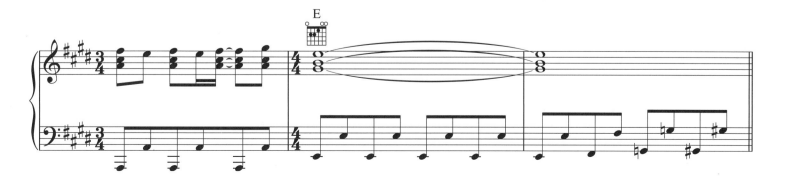

# GOODBYE YELLOW BRICK ROAD

Words and Music by ELTON JOHN
and BERNIE TAUPIN

When are you gon-na come down? When are you going to land?
What do you think you'll do then? I bet that'll shoot down your plane.

I should have stayed on the farm. I should have
It'll take you a cou-ple of vod-ka and ton-ics to

lis-tened to my old man. You know you can't hold me for-ev-
set you on your feet a-gain. May-be you'll get a re-place-

# HELLO, IT'S ME

Words and Music by
TODD RUNDGREN

Lyrics:

Hel - lo, __ it's me.

I thought a - bout __ us for a long, __ long time. __

May - be I think too much but some-thing's wrong. __

There's some-thing here does-n't last too long. __

May - be I should-n't think of

# HOTEL CALIFORNIA

Words and Music by DON HENLEY,
GLENN FREY and DON FELDER

**Moderate Rock**

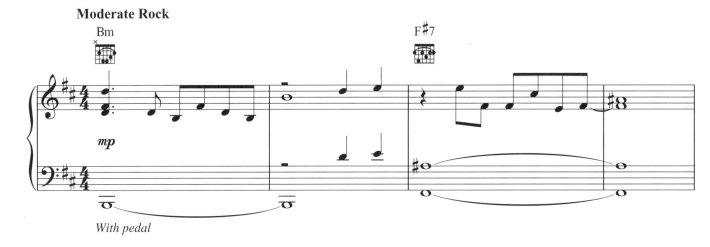

*With pedal*

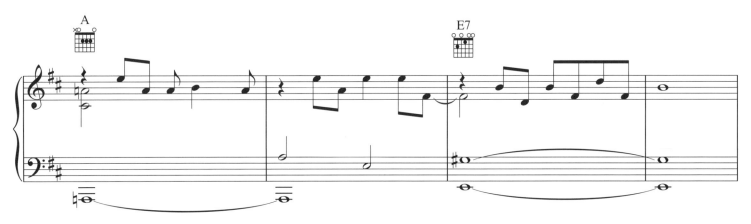

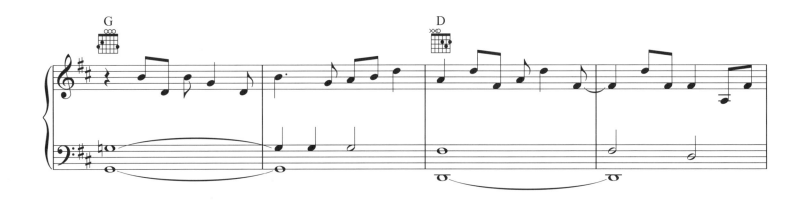

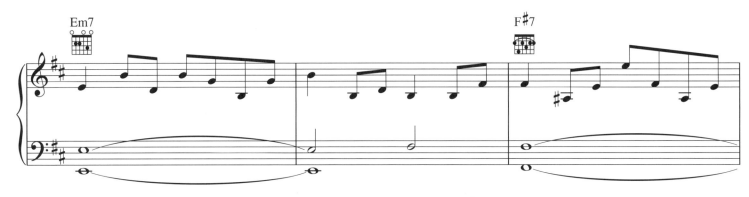

164

# HOW DEEP IS YOUR LOVE

Words and Music by BARRY GIBB,
ROBIN GIBB and MAURICE GIBB

# I AM WOMAN

Words by HELEN REDDY
Music by RAY BURTON

**Moderate Rock beat**

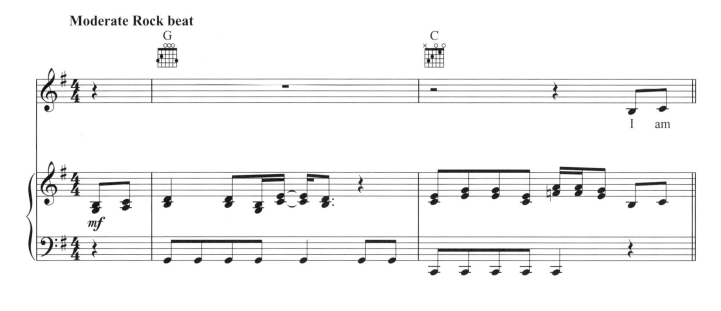

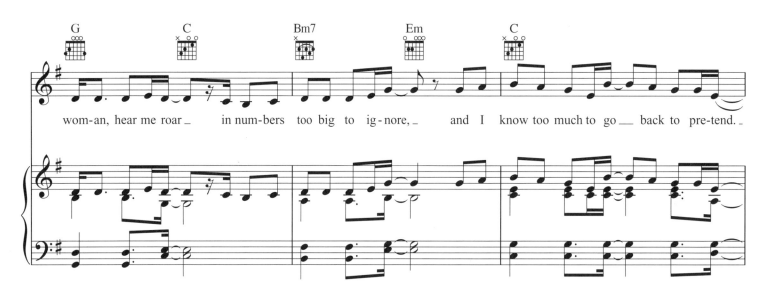

# I SHOT THE SHERIFF

Words and Music by
BOB MARLEY

Moderately slow, with a beat

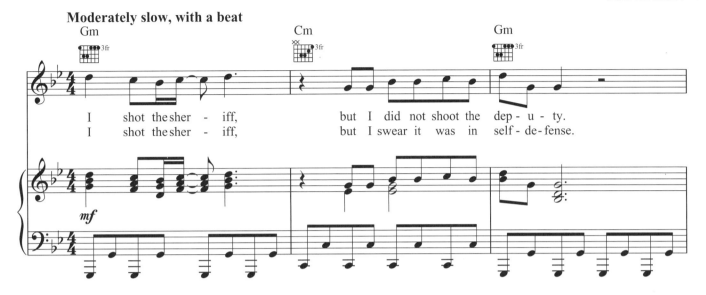

I shot the sher - iff, but I did not shoot the dep - u - ty.
I shot the sher - iff, but I swear it was in self - de - fense.

I shot the sher - iff, but I did - n't shoot the
I shot the sher - iff, and they say it is a

dep - u - ty.
cap - i - tal of - fense.

All a - round in my
Sher - iff John Brown al - ways

# I CAN SEE CLEARLY NOW

Words and Music by
JOHNNY NASH

Look all a-round,_____ there's noth-ing but blue skies._____

_____ Look straight a-head,_____ noth-ing but

blue skies._____

# I WILL SURVIVE

Words and Music by DINO FEKARIS
and FREDERICK J. PERREN

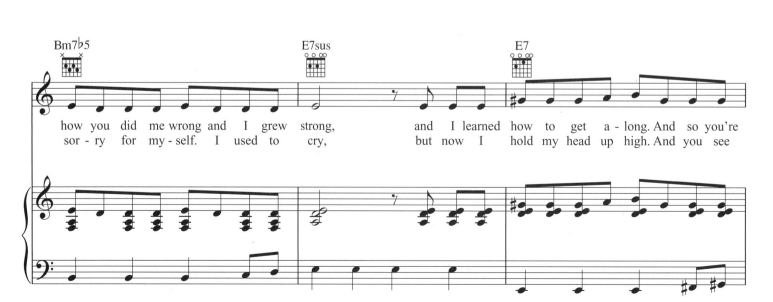

# KILLING ME SOFTLY WITH HIS SONG

Words by NORMAN GIMBEL
Music by CHARLES FOX

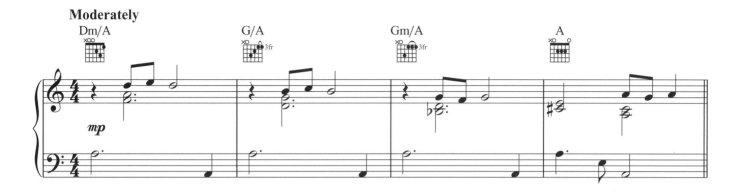

I heard _ he sang _ a good _ song,
I felt _ all flushed _ with fe - ver,
He sang _ as if _ he knew _ me

I heard he had _
em - bar - rassed by _
in all my dark _

_ a style,
_ the crowd.
_ de - spair.

and so _ I came _ to see _ him to
I felt _ he came found my let - ters and
And then _ he looked _ right through _ me as

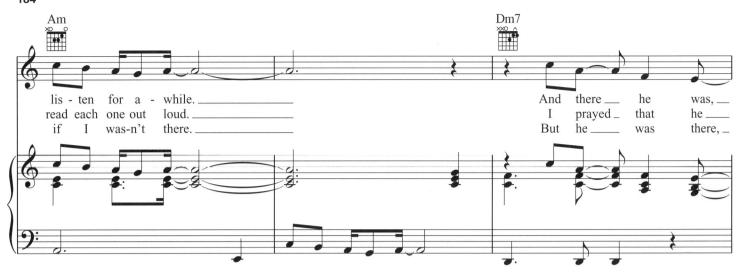

lis - ten for a - while. ____ And there __ he was, __
read each one out loud. ____ I prayed __ that he __
if I was-n't there. ____ But he __ was there, __

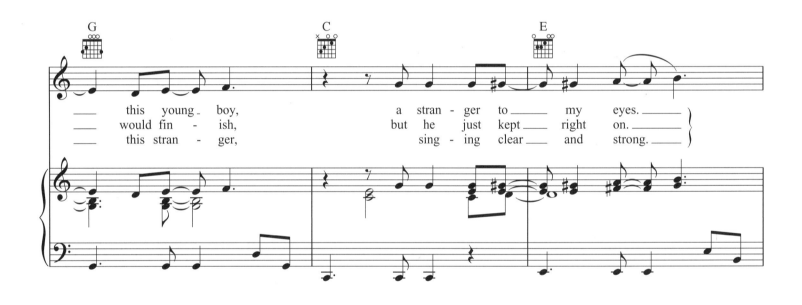

__ this young __ boy, a stran - ger to __ my eyes. ____
__ would fin - ish, but he just kept __ right on. ____
__ this stran - ger, sing - ing clear __ and strong. ____

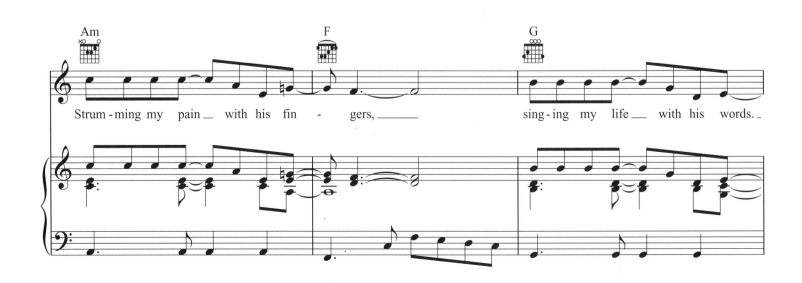

Strum - ming my pain __ with his fin - gers, ____ sing-ing my life __ with his words. __

# I WISH

Words and Music by
STEVIE WONDER

**Bright Funk**

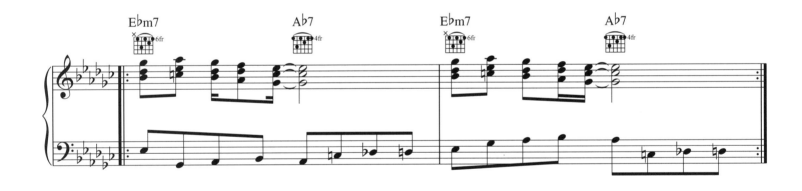

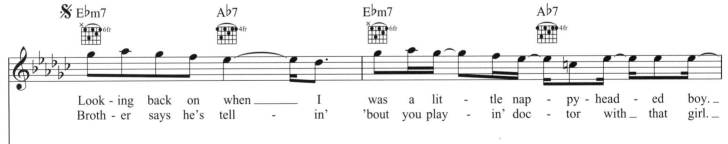

Look - ing back on when _____ I was a lit - tle nap - py - head - ed boy.
Broth - er says he's tell - in' 'bout you play - in' doc - tor with __ that girl.

D.S. al Coda

do  do __  do  do __  do      do  do  do  do  do. __

er  have __  to  go.

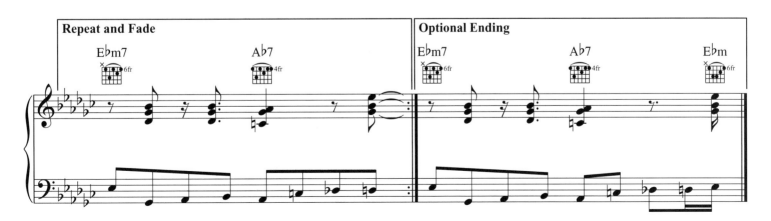

**Repeat and Fade**

**Optional Ending**

# I WRITE THE SONGS

Words and Music by
BRUCE JOHNSTON

# IF

Words and Music by
DAVID GATES

**Moderately, with feeling**

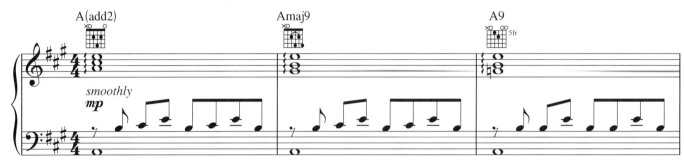

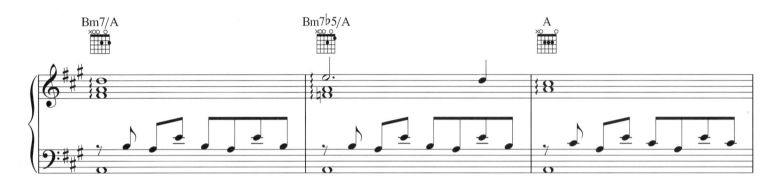

If a

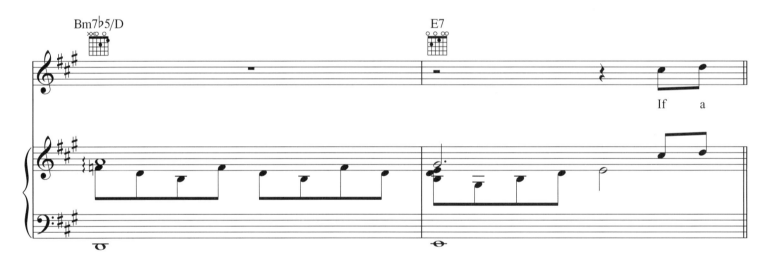

pic - ture paints a thou - sand words, __ then why __
man could be two plac - es at __ one time, __

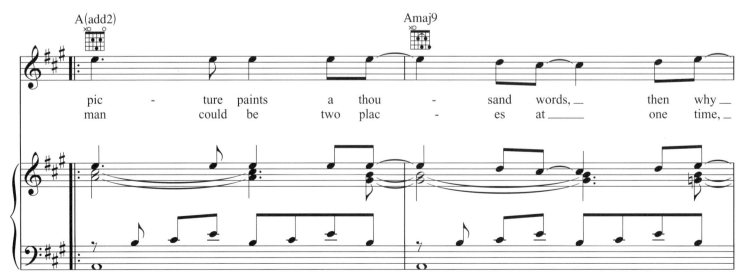

199

# IMAGINE

Words and Music by
JOHN LENNON

202

# IT'S TOO LATE

Words and Music by CAROLE KING
and TONI STERN

it, oh, ___ no, ___ no, ___ no, ___ no, ___ no, ___ no.

no, ___ no, ___

There'll be good times ___ a-gain for me and ___ you, ___ but we just can't stay to-geth - er; don't you

# JOY TO THE WORLD

Words and Music by
HOYT AXTON

# LADY MARMALADE

Words and Music by BOB CREWE
and KENNY NOLAN

# LAY DOWN SALLY

Words and Music by ERIC CLAPTON,
MARCY LEVY and GEORGE TERRY

**Bright beat**

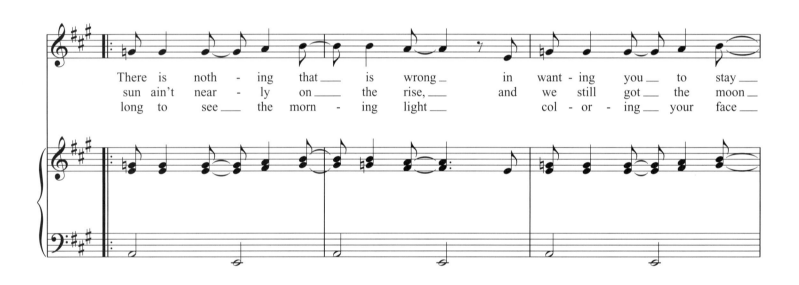

There is noth-ing that __ is wrong __ in want-ing you __ to stay __
sun ain't near-ly on __ the rise, __ and we still got __ the moon __
long to see __ the morn-ing light __ col-or-ing __ your face __

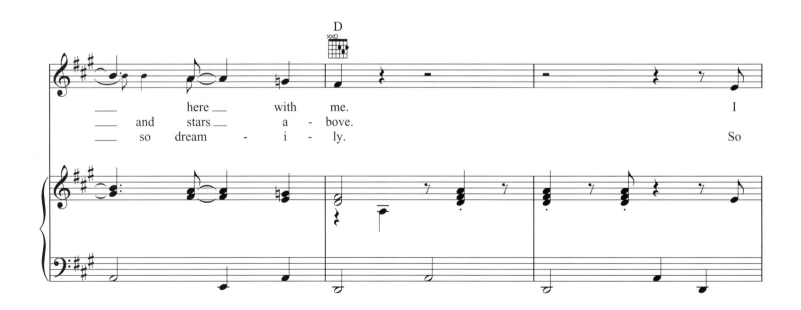

__ here __ with me.   I
__ and stars __ a - bove.   So
__ so dream - i - ly.

Don't you think __ you want __ some-one __ to talk __ to?

Lay down, Sal - ly; __ no

need to leave __ so soon. __ I've been try - ing all __

__ night long __ just to talk to you. __

To Coda
1, 2

The talk to you. ___
I

D.S. al Coda

CODA

talk to you. ___

Repeat and Fade

# LAYLA

Words and Music by ERIC CLAPTON
and JIM GORDON

**Medium fast Rock**

What will you do___ when you get lone-ly
I tried___ to give___ you con-so-___ la-tion
So make___ the best___ of the sit-u-___ a-tion

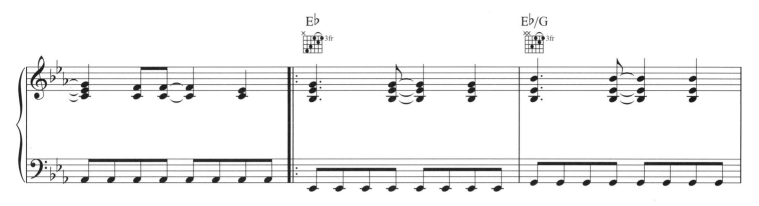

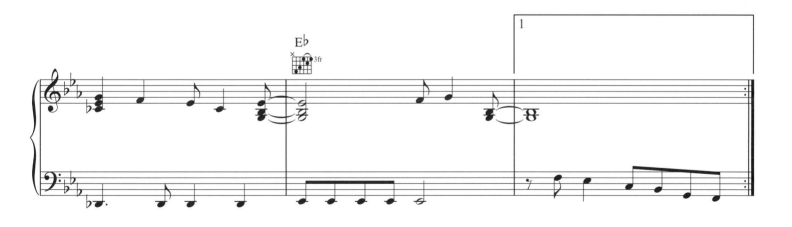

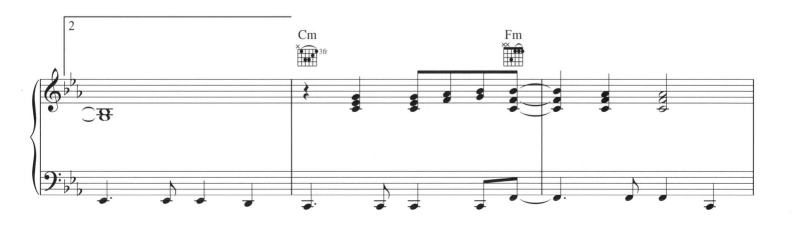

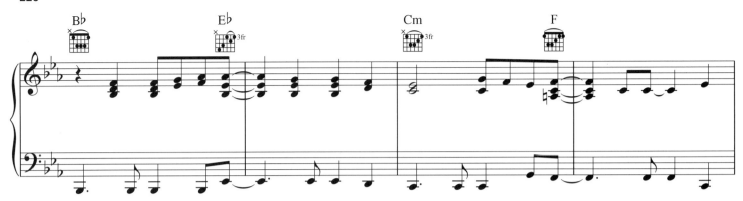

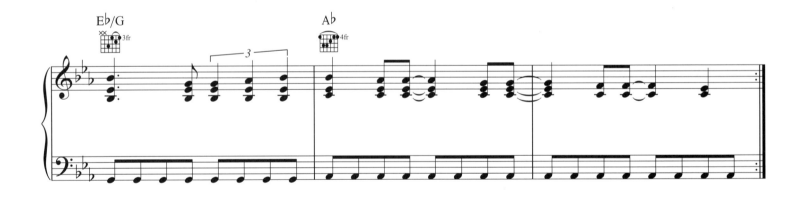

**Freely**

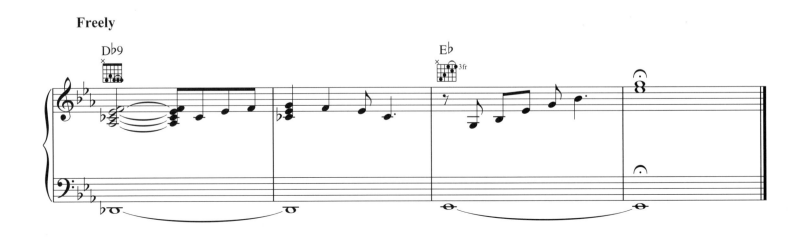

# LE FREAK

Words and Music by NILE RODGERS
and BERNARD EDWARDS

**Medium Disco beat**

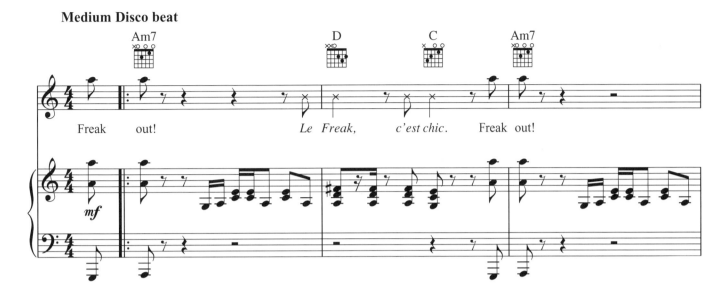

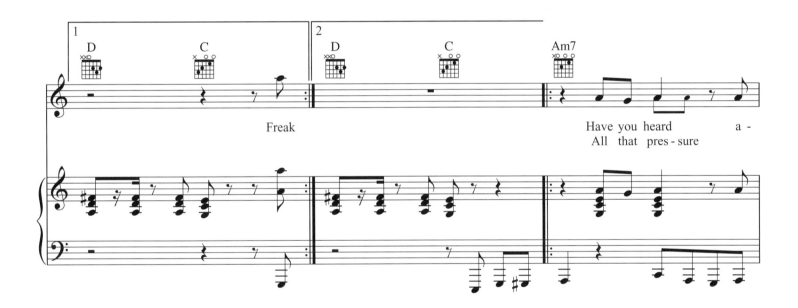

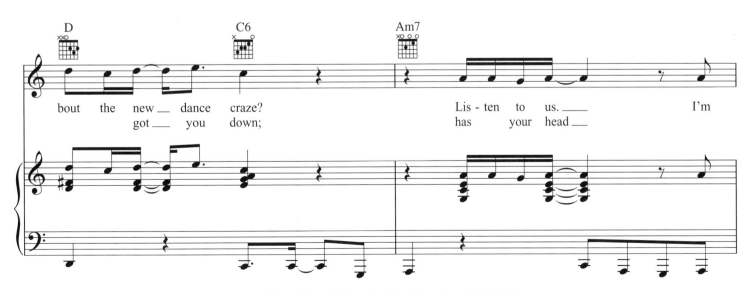

# LEAN ON ME

Words and Music by
BILL WITHERS

Some - times in our lives, _____ we all have pain, _____

232

# LET IT BE

Words and Music by JOHN LENNON
and PAUL McCARTNEY

When I find my-self __ in times of trou - ble,
*Instrumental*

Moth - er Mar - y comes to me speak-ing words of wis - dom; let it

be. _____ And in my hour of dark - ness, she is

240

# LET'S GET IT ON

Words and Music by MARVIN GAYE
and ED TOWNSEND

**Slow Soul beat**

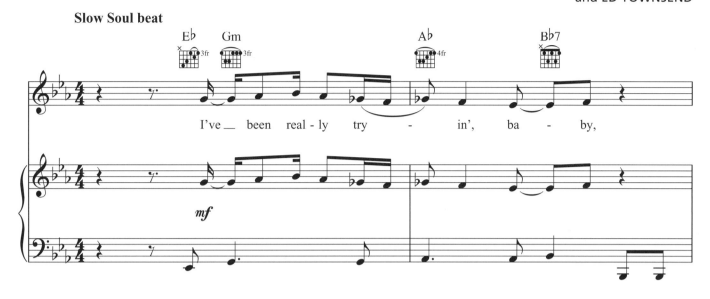

I've __ been real-ly try - in', ba - by,

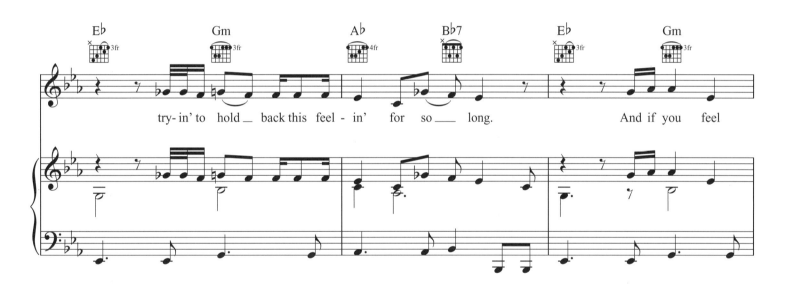

try-in' to hold __ back this feel - in' for so __ long. And if you feel

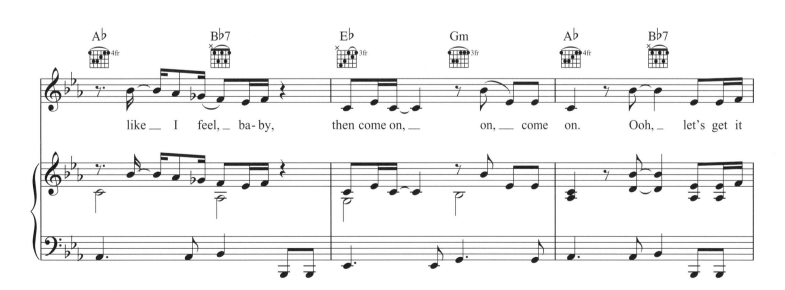

like __ I feel, __ ba - by, then come on, __ on, __ come on. Ooh, __ let's get it

# LOVE WILL KEEP US TOGETHER

Words and Music by NEIL SEDAKA
and HOWARD GREENFIELD

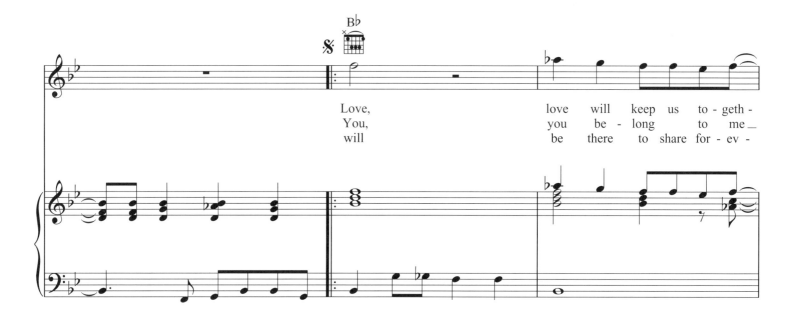

# MAGGIE MAY

Words and Music by ROD STEWART
and MARTIN QUITTENTON

258

*Additional Lyrics*

2. You lured me away from home, just to save you from being alone.
You stole my soul, that's a pain I can do without.
All I needed was a friend to lend a guiding hand.
But you turned into a lover, and, mother, what a lover! You wore me out.
All you did was wreck my bed and in the morning kick me in the head.
Oh, Maggie, I couldn't have tried anymore.

3. You lured me away from home 'cause you didn't want to be alone.
You stole my heart, I couldn't leave you if I tried.
I suppose I could collect my books and get back to school,
Or steal my daddy's cue and make a living out of playing pool,
Or find myself a rock and roll band that needs a helpin' hand.
Oh, Maggie, I wish I'd never seen your face. *(To Coda)*

# MANDY

Words and Music by SCOTT ENGLISH
and RICHARD KERR

# MAYBE I'M AMAZED

Words and Music by
PAUL McCARTNEY

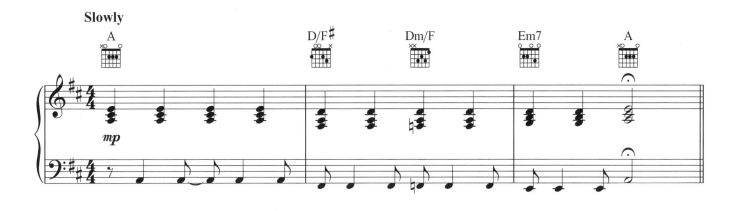

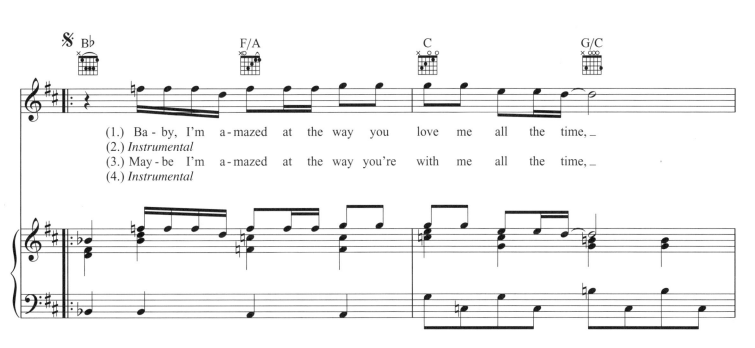

(1.) Ba - by, I'm a - mazed at the way you love me all the time,_
(2.) *Instrumental*
(3.) May - be I'm a - mazed at the way you're with me all the time,_
(4.) *Instrumental*

and may - be I'm a - fraid of the way I love you.

and may - be I'm a - fraid of the way I need you.

Bb    F/A    C    G

May - be I'm a - mazed at the way you pulled me out of time, _ you
May - be I'm a - mazed at the way you help me sing my song, _ you

Bb    F/A    Ab    Eb/G    C    **To Coda** ⊕

hung me on a line. ___ May-be I'm a - mazed at the way I real - ly need you.
right me when I'm wrong. _ May-be I'm a - mazed at the way I real - ly need you. _

*Instrumental ends*

D    A/D    Am/D    D9/F#

(1.,2.) Ba - by, I'm a man, may-be I'm a lone - ly man _ who's in the mid-dle of some - thing _
(3.) *Vocal ad lib.*

G    D(add#9)

that he does-n't real - ly un - der - stand. _____

# MERCY, MERCY ME
## (The Ecology)

Words and Music by
MARVIN GAYE

# MONEY

Words and Music by
ROGER WATERS

Mon-ey,
Mon-ey,
Mon-ey,

ya get a-
you get
it's a

way.
back.
crime.

Ya get a good job with more pay, and you're O my
I'm all right, Jack. Keep your hands off my
Share it fair-ly, but don't take a slice of

- K.
_____ stack.
my _____ pie.

Mon - ey,
Mon - ey,
Mon - ey,

it's a
it's a
so they

gas.
hit.
say,

Grab that cash with both hands and make _
But don't give me that do - good - y good bull _
is the root of all e - vil to -

_____ a stash.
- shit.
- day.

I'm in the
But if

New car, cav - i - ar, four - star day - dream.
high fi - del - i - ty, first - class trav - 'ling
you ask for __ a raise, it's no sur -

F#m

# MOONDANCE

Words and Music by
VAN MORRISON

Moderately

(1.) Well, it's a
(2.) wan - na make love ____ to you to -
(3.) mar - vel - ous night ____ for a moon-

- dance with the stars up a - bove in your eyes. ____ A fan -
- night, I can't wait till the morn - ing has come. ____ And I

tab - u - lous night ____ to make ro - mance 'neath the cov - er of Oc - to - ber skies.
know now the time ____ is just ____ right and straight in - to my arms ____ you will run.

# MY EYES ADORED YOU

Words and Music by BOB CREWE
and KENNY NOLAN

Moderately slow

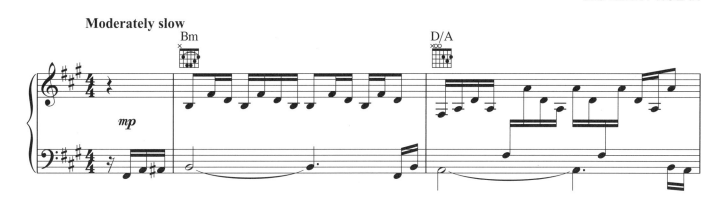

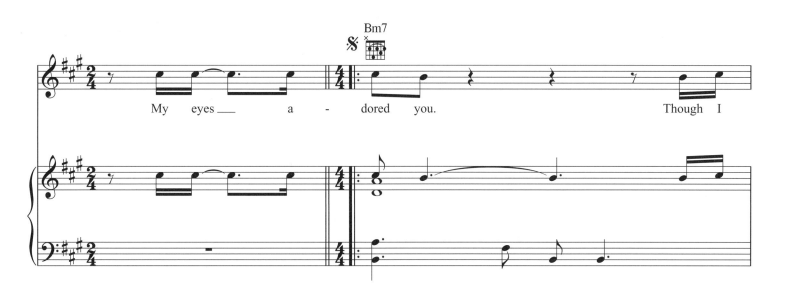

My eyes ___ a - dored you.

Though I

# MY LOVE

Words and Music by PAUL McCARTNEY
and LINDA McCARTNEY

And when I go a - way, __ I know my heart can stay __ with my
And when the cup-board's bare, __ I'll still find some-thing there __ with my
Don't ev - er ask me why __ I nev - er said good-bye __ to my

love.
love. } It's un - der - stood. __ It's in the hands __ of my love, _____ and
love.

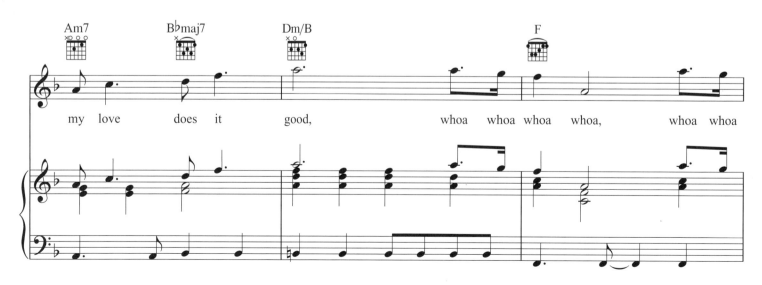

my love does it good, whoa whoa whoa whoa, whoa whoa

# MY SHARONA

Words and Music by DOUG FIEGER
and BERTON AVERRE

G7(no3)
you make my mo - tor run, my mo - tor run. Gun
- in' it a mys - ter - y, it gets to me. Run -
it d - d - des - ti - ny, d - des - ti - ny, or
C
Bb
it com - in' off of the line, Sha - ro - na.
- nin' down the length of my thigh, Sha - ro - na. Nev -
is it just a game in my mind, Sha - ro - na?
G7(no3)
Bb
- er gon - na stop, give it up. Such a dirt - y mind. I al - ways get it up for the
To Coda
C
Eb
3fr
F5
touch of the young - er kind. My, my, my, iy, iy, woo!

*End solo*

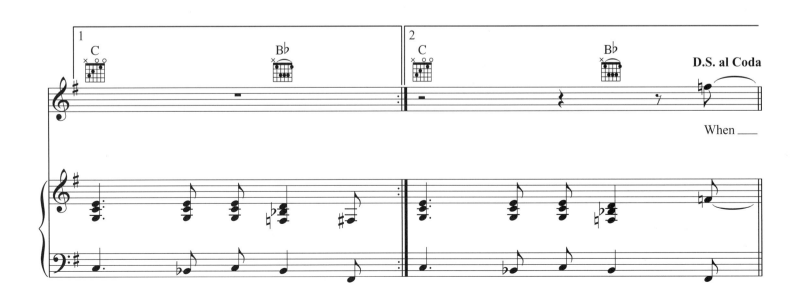

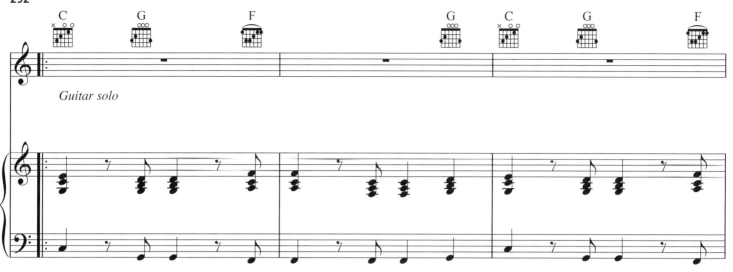

*Guitar solo*

**Repeat ad lib.**

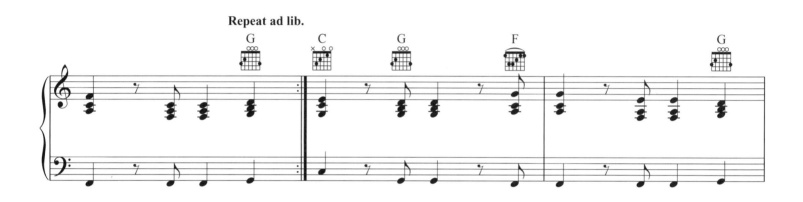

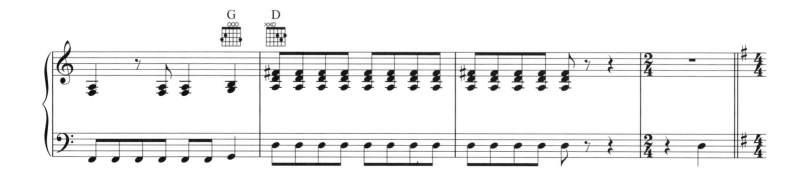

# NIGHTS IN WHITE SATIN

Words and Music by
JUSTIN HAYWARD

# PIANO MAN

Words and Music by
BILLY JOEL

# PAPA WAS A ROLLIN' STONE

Words and Music by NORMAN WHITFIELD
and BARRETT STRONG

**Moderately fast**

It was the third of Sep - tem - ber.

nev - er got a chance to see ___

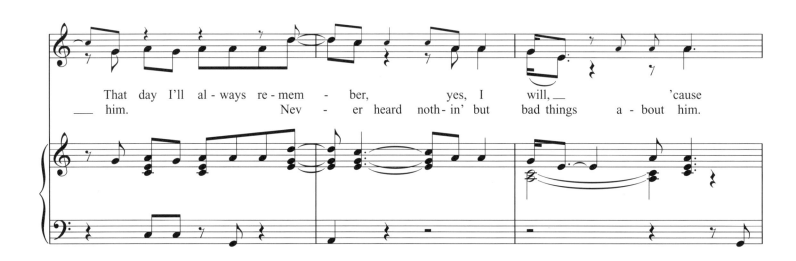

That day I'll al - ways re - mem - ber, yes, I will, ___ 'cause

___ him. Nev - er heard noth - in' but bad things a - bout him.

that was the day \_\_\_\_ that my dad - dy died. \_\_\_\_\_
Ma - ma, I'm de - pend - ing on you to tell me the truth. \_

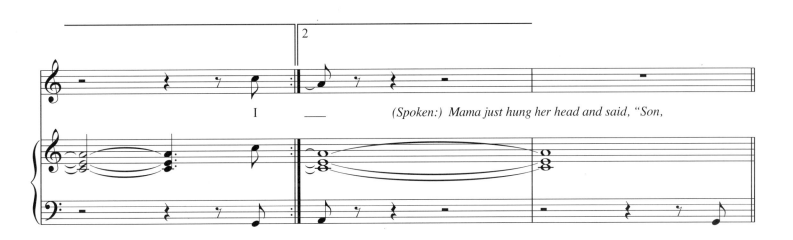

I \_\_\_ *(Spoken:) Mama just hung her head and said, "Son,*

Pa - pa was a roll - in' stone." \_ Wher - ev - er he laid his hat

was his home. \_ And when he died, \_ all \_\_\_\_ he \_\_\_ left us was a -

# PUT YOUR HAND IN THE HAND

Words and Music by
GENE MacLELLAN

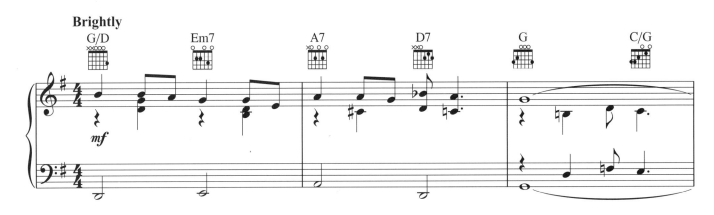

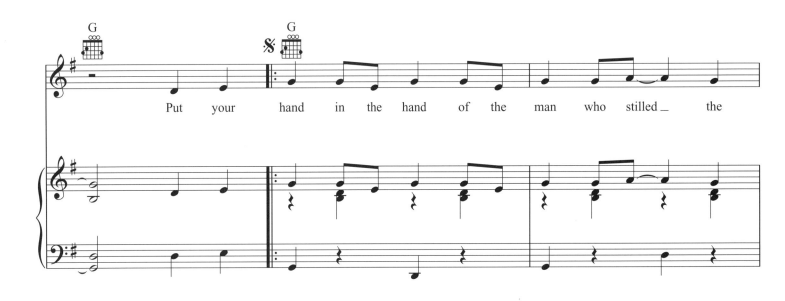

Put your hand in the hand of the man who stilled __ the wa - ter. _____

Put your hand in the hand of the

# THE RAINBOW CONNECTION

Words and Music by PAUL WILLIAMS
and KENNETH L. ASCHER

Why are there so man-y songs a-bout rain-bows, and
Who said that ev-'ry wish would be heard and an-swered when

what's on the oth - er side? _____
wished on the morn - ing star? _____

Rain - bows are vi - sions, __ but on - ly il - lu - sions, and
Some - bod - y thought of that, and some - one be - lieved it;

# RAINDROPS KEEP FALLIN' ON MY HEAD

## from BUTCH CASSIDY AND THE SUNDANCE KID

Lyric by HAL DAVID
Music by BURT BACHARACH

# REELING IN THE YEARS

Words and Music by WALTER BECKER
and DONALD FAGEN

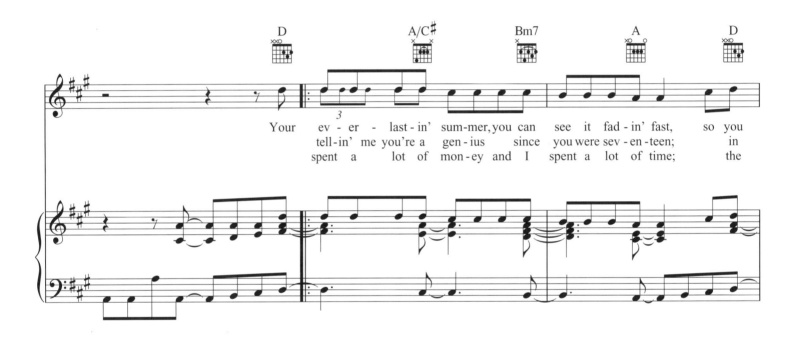

Your ev-er-last-in' sum-mer, you can see it fad-in' fast, so you
tell-in' me you're a gen-ius since you were sev-en-teen; in
spent a lot of mon-ey and I spent a lot of time; the

grab a piece of some-thin' that you think is gon-na last. Well, you
all the time I've known you I still don't know what you mean. The
trip we made to Hol-ly-wood is etched up-on my mind. Af-ter

# REUNITED

Words and Music by DINO FEKARIS
and FREDDIE PERREN

one per-fect fit ___ and, sug-ar, this one is it. ___ We both are so ex-cit-ed, 'cause we're

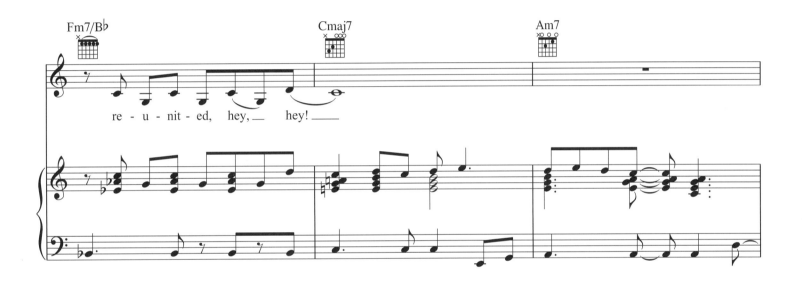

re-u-nit-ed, hey, ___ hey! ___

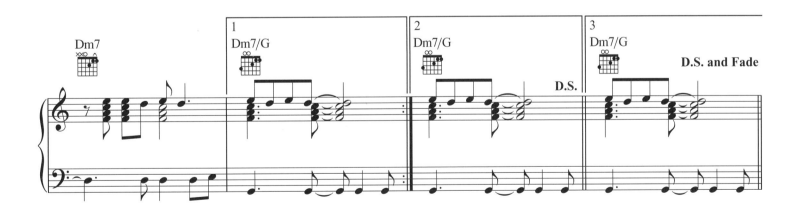

*Additional Lyrics*

4. Ooh, listen, baby, I won't ever make you cry, I won't let one day go by
Without holding you, without kissing you, without loving you.
Ooh, you're my everything, only you know how to free
All the love there is in me.
I wanna let you know, I won't let you go.
I wanna let you know, I won't let you go.
Ooh, feels so good!

# ROCKET MAN
## (I Think It's Gonna Be a Long Long Time)

Words and Music by ELTON JOHN
and BERNIE TAUPIN

**Moderate Ballad**

She packed_ my bags_ last night pre - flight,_

ze - ro ho - ur, nine A. M._____

And I'm gon - na be high _____ as a kite by

329

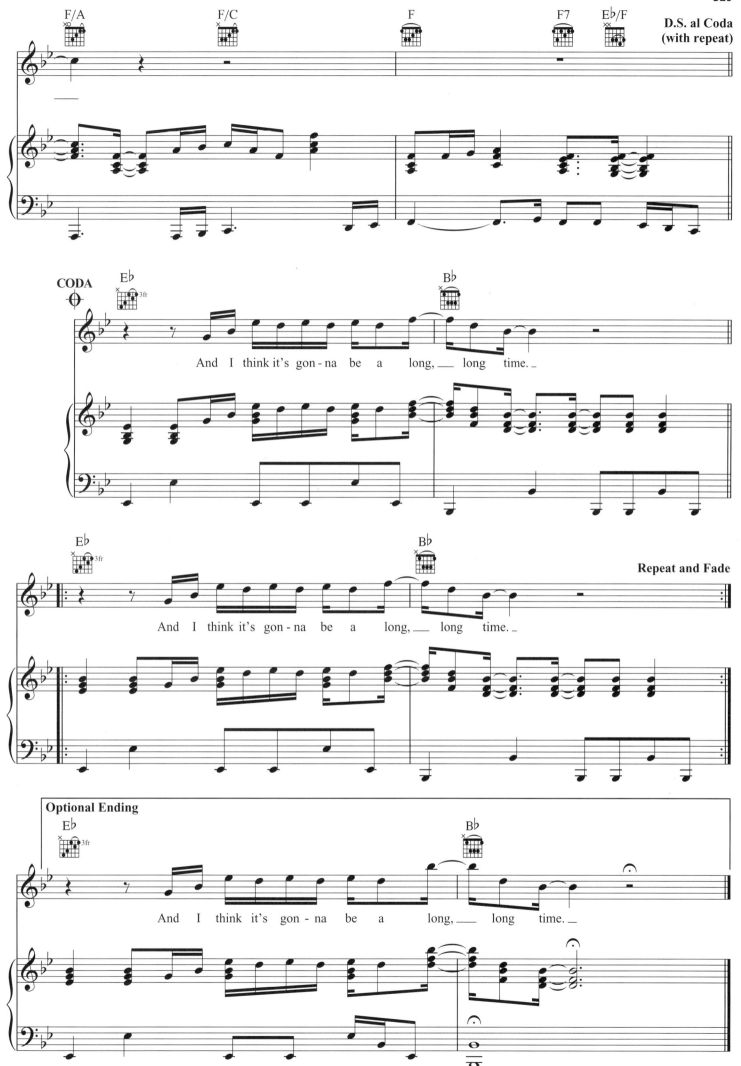

# SEPTEMBER

Words and Music by MAURICE WHITE,
AL McKAY and ALLEE WILLIS

**Moderate Rock**

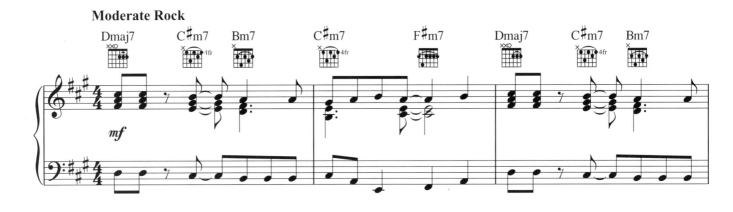

1. Do you re - mem - ber
ring - ing in the key ___
3., 4. (*See additional lyrics*)

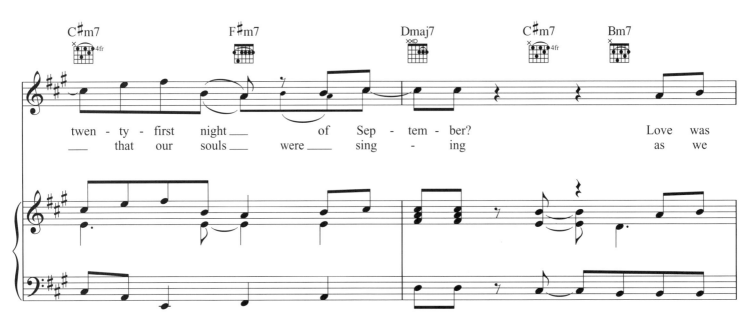

twen-ty-first night ___ of Sep - tem - ber? Love was
___ that our souls ___ were ___ sing - ing as we

*Additional Lyrics*

3. My thoughts are with you,
   Holding hands with your heart,
   To see you, only blue talk and love.
   Remember how we knew love was here to stay?

4. Now December found the love that we shared,
   September, only blue talk and love.
   Remember the true love we share today.
   *Chorus*

# THEME FROM SHAFT

## from SHAFT

Words and Music by
ISAAC HAYES

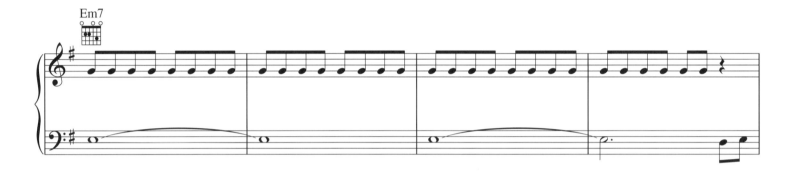

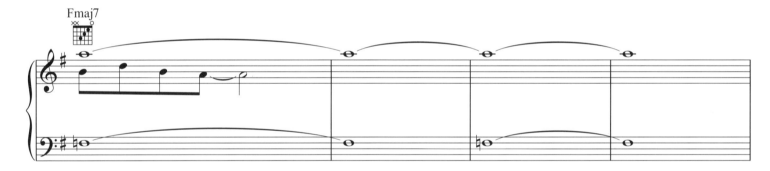

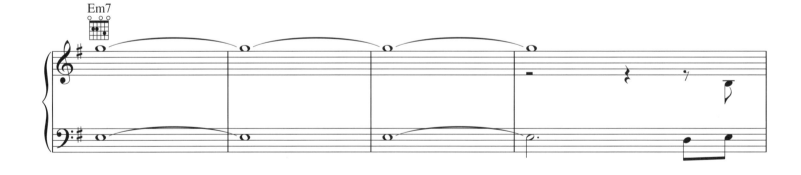

(Spoken:) Who's the black pri - vate dick __ that's a sex ma - chine to all the chicks?   (Shaft!)

*You're damn right!*

Who   is the man   that would   risk his life for his broth-er   man? __   (Shaft!)

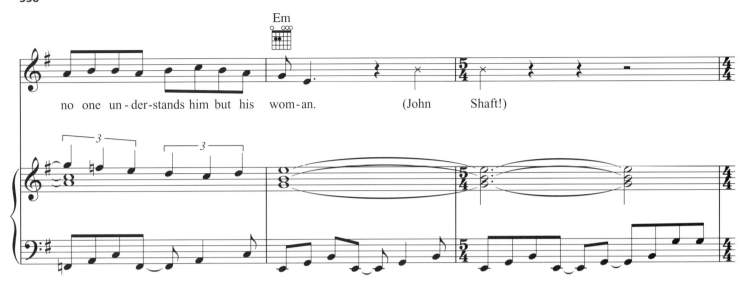

no one un-der-stands him but his wom-an. (John Shaft!)

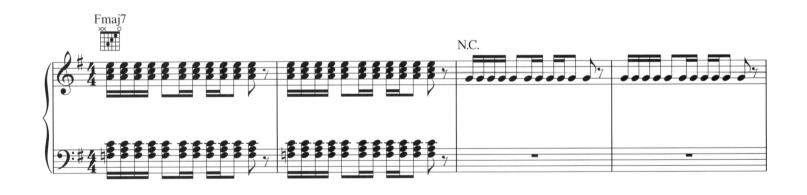

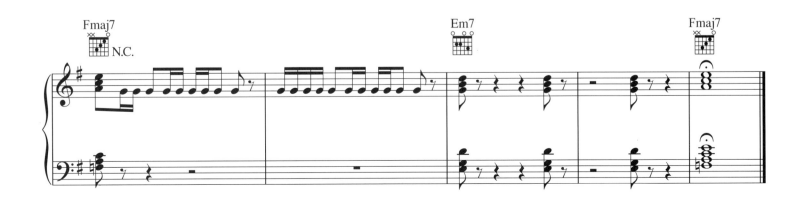

# SHE'S ALWAYS A WOMAN

Words and Music by
BILLY JOEL

340

D.S. al Coda

most she will do is throw shad-ows at you. But she's al-ways a wom-an to

me. _____ Hmm _____ Hmm _

# SMOKE ON THE WATER

Words and Music by RITCHIE BLACKMORE,
IAN GILLAN, ROGER GLOVER,
JON LORD and IAN PAICE

We all came out to Mon-
They burned down the gam-
We end-ed up at the Grand

- treux on the Lake Ge-ne-va shore-line,
bling house, it died with an aw-ful sound.
Ho-tel, It was emp-ty cold and bare, but with the

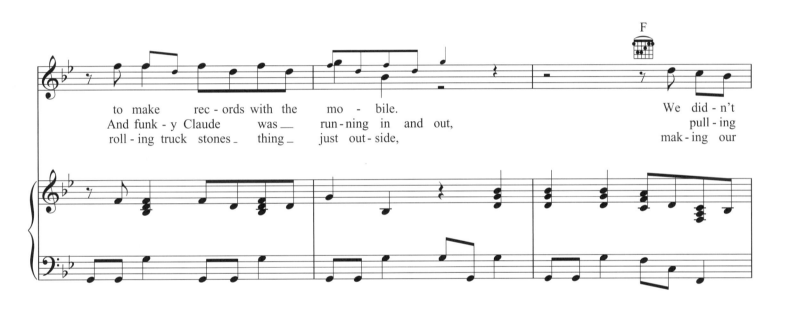

to make rec-ords with the mo-bile. We did-n't
And funk-y Claude was run-ning in and out, pull-ing
roll-ing truck stones thing just out-side, mak-ing our

have much time. Frank Zap-pa and the Moth-ers were
kids out the ground. When it all was o-ver, we
mu-sic there. With a few red lights, a few old beds,

**Repeat and Fade**

**Optional Ending**

# SONG SUNG BLUE

Words and Music by
NEIL DIAMOND

and be-fore you know it start to feel-in' good. _ You sim-ply got no choice. _

# STAYIN' ALIVE

Words and Music by BARRY GIBB,
ROBIN GIBB and MAURICE GIBB

Repeat and Fade

# STAIRWAY TO HEAVEN

Words and Music by JIMMY PAGE
and ROBERT PLANT

There's a la - dy who's sure _ all that glit - ters is gold, _ and she's

your stair-way lies on the whis - p'ring wind? _____ Oh. _____

**Faster**

# SUMMER BREEZE

Words and Music by JAMES SEALS
and DASH CROFTS

# SUPERSTITION

Words and Music by
STEVIE WONDER

# SWEET HOME ALABAMA

Words and Music by RONNIE VAN ZANT,
ED KING and GARY ROSSINGTON

Moderately slow

# TIN MAN

Words and Music by
DEWEY BUNNELL

**Fast**

Some - times __ late __ when things are real and __ peo -

- ple share the gift of __ gab __ be - tween them -

# TAKE ME HOME, COUNTRY ROADS

Words and Music by JOHN DENVER,
BILL DANOFF and TAFFY NIVERT

# TIE A YELLOW RIBBON ROUND THE OLE OAK TREE

Words and Music by L. RUSSELL BROWN
and IRWIN LEVINE

# TIME IN A BOTTLE

Words and Music by
JIM CROCE

# TOP OF THE WORLD

Words and Music by JOHN BETTIS
and RICHARD CARPENTER

Such a feel - in's com - in' o - ver me. ___
Some - thing in ___ the wind has learned ___ my name. ___

# The Way We Were

Words by ALAN and MARILYN BERGMAN
Music by MARVIN HAMLISCH

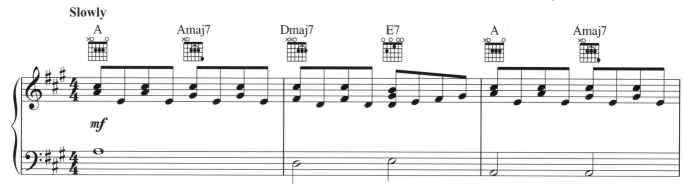

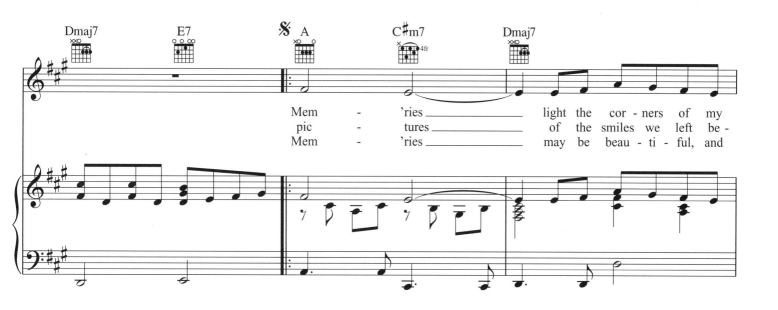

Mem - 'ries _____ light the cor - ners of my
pic - tures _____ of the smiles we left be -
Mem - 'ries _____ may be beau - ti - ful, and

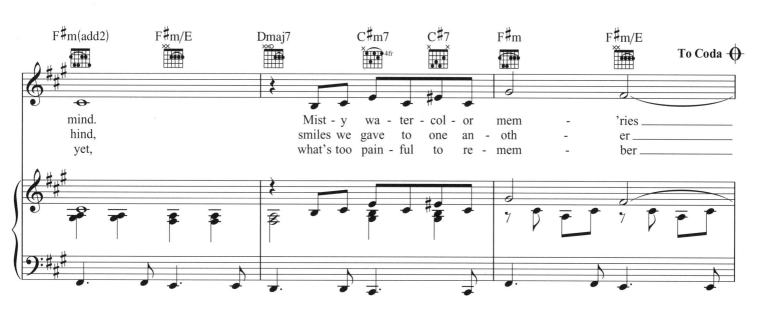

mind.
hind,          smiles we gave to one an - oth - er _____
yet,           what's too pain - ful to re - mem - ber _____

Mist - y wa - ter - col - or mem - 'ries _____

# 25 OR 6 TO 4

Words and Music by
ROBERT LAMM

**Bright Rock**

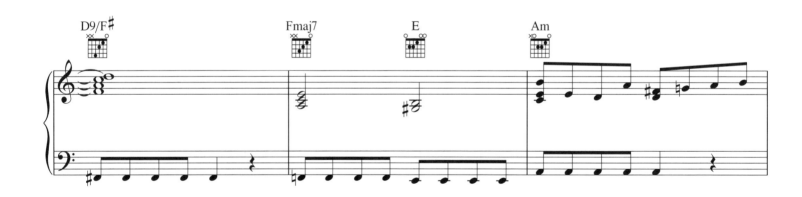

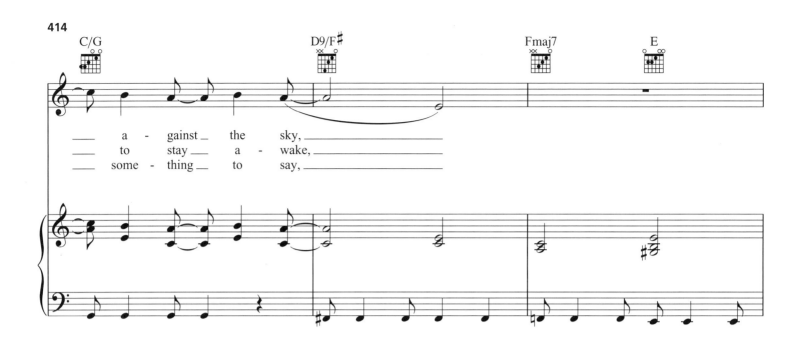

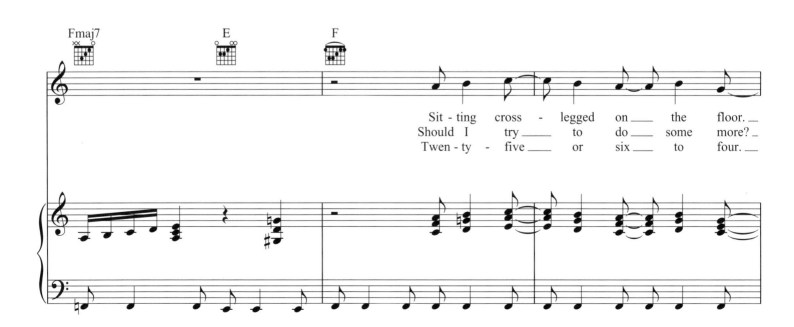

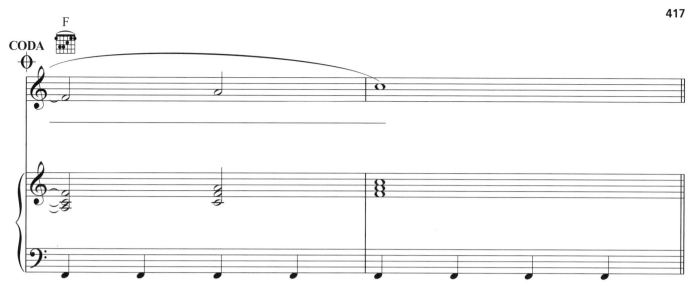

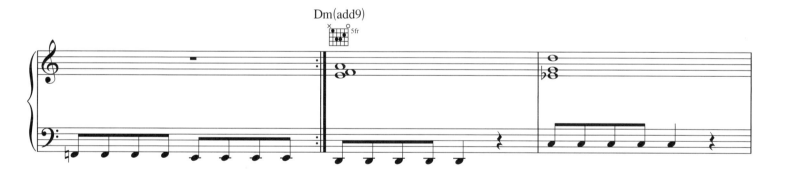

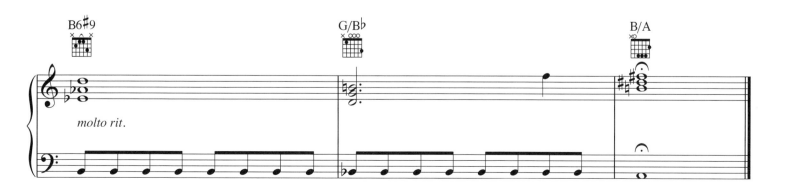

# WALK THIS WAY

Words and Music by STEVEN TYLER
and JOE PERRY

**Back**-stroke lov-er al-ways hid-in' 'neath the cov-ers 'til I talked to your dad-dy, he say; ___

**School**-girl sweet-ies with a class-y, kind-a sass-y lit-tle skirts climb-in' way up their knees; ___

___ he said, "You ain't seen noth-in' 'til you're down on a muf-fin, then you're

___ there was ___ three young la-dies in the school gym ___ lock-er when I

sure to be chang-ing your ways." ___      I meet a cheer - lead - er, was a
no - ticed they was look - in' at me. ___      I was a high school los - er, nev - er

real young bleed - er; oh, the times I could rem - i - nisce, ___      'cause the
made it with a la - dy till the boys told me some - thing I missed. ___      Then my

best things of lov - in' with her sis - ter and her cous - in on - ly start - ed with a lit - tle kiss, ___
next - door ___ neigh-bor with a daugh-ter had a fa - vor, so I gave her just a lit - tle kiss, ___

G5    A5

N.C.

___ like this: )
___ like this: )

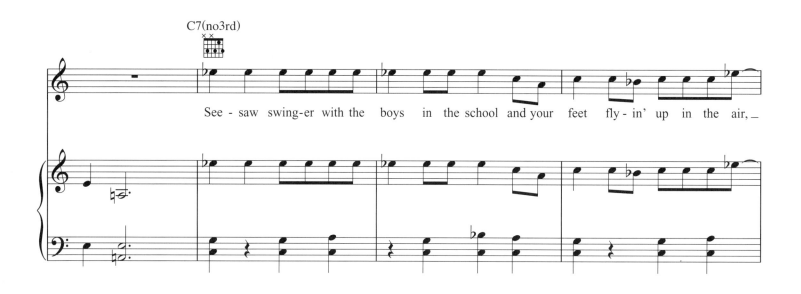

See - saw swing-er with the boys in the school and your feet fly - in' up in the air,

sing - ing, "Hey, did - dle, did - dle," with your kit - ty in the mid - dle of the

swing like you did - n't care. So I took a big chance at the

walk this — way, — walk this — way, —

walk this — way, — walk this — way, —

walk this — way. — Just give me a kiss. *Guitar solo ad lib.*

# WE ARE FAMILY

Words and Music by NILE RODGERS
and BERNARD EDWARDS

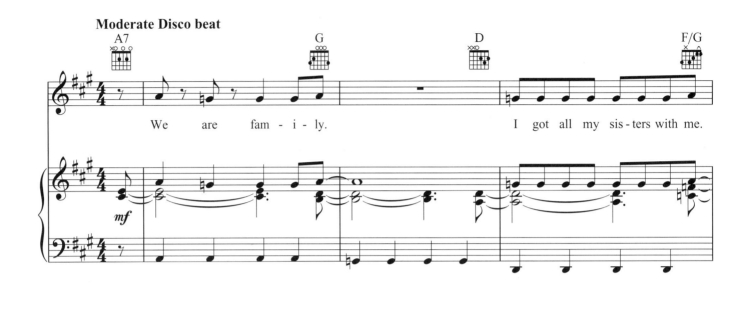

# WE'VE ONLY JUST BEGUN

Words and Music by ROGER NICHOLS
and PAUL WILLIAMS

**Slowly**

We've on-ly just be-gun _____ to live. _____

_____ White lace and prom - is - es, a kiss for luck _ and we're

on our way. _____

(1.) Be - fore the ris - ing
(2., D.S.) And when the eve - ning

# WE WILL ROCK YOU

Words and Music by
BRIAN MAY

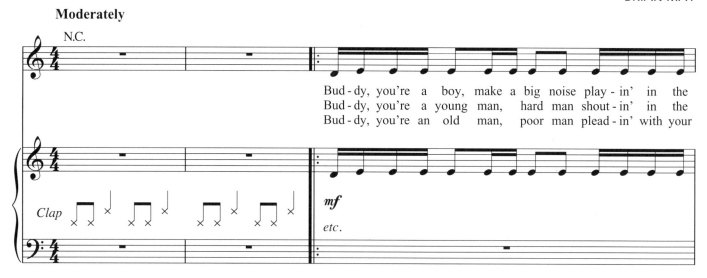

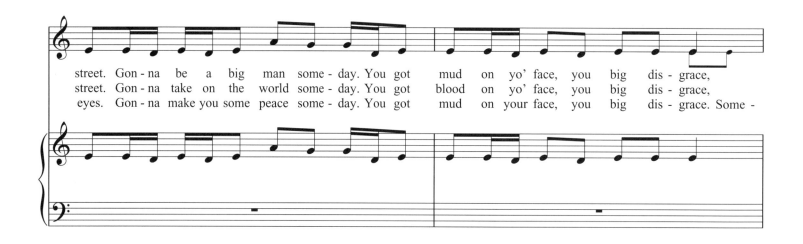

# WISH YOU WERE HERE

Words and Music by ROGER WATERS
and DAVID GILMOUR

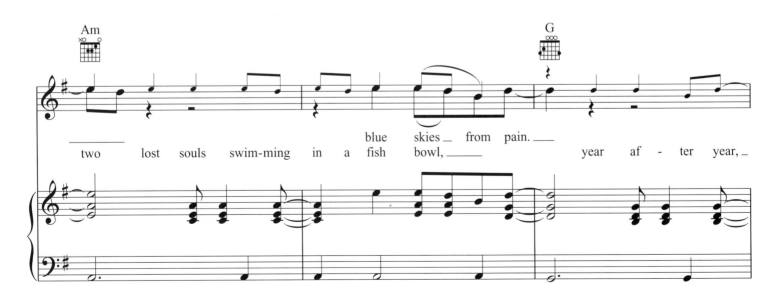

Da da da da      da da da da da.

# YOU ARE THE SUNSHINE OF MY LIFE

Words and Music by
STEVIE WONDER

# Y.M.C.A.

Words and Music by JACQUES MORALI,
HENRI BELOLO and VICTOR WILLIS

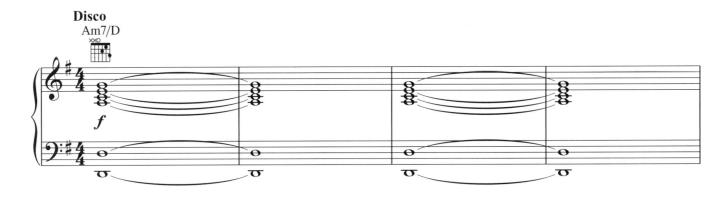

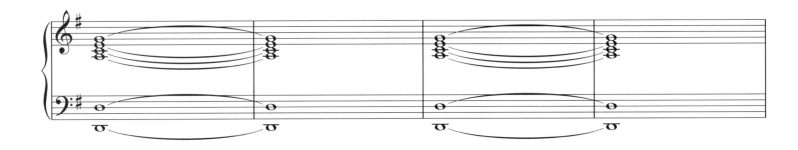

1.Young man,          there's no

2., 3. *(See additional lyrics)*

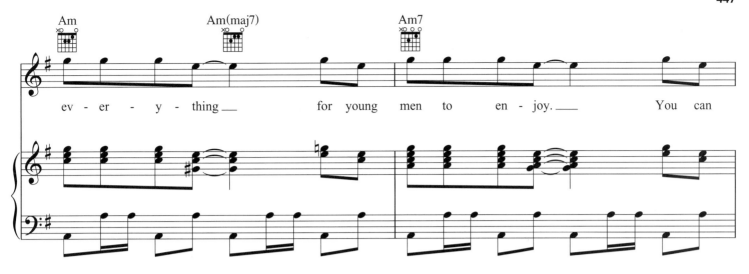

ev - er - y - thing ___ for young men to en - joy. ___ You can

**Repeat ad lib. and Fade**

hang out with all ___ the boys. ___ It's fun to stay at the

*Additional Lyrics*

2. Young man, are you listening to me?
I said, young man, what do you want to be?
I said, young man, you can make real your dreams
But you've got to know this one thing.

No man does it all by himself.
I said, young man, put your pride on the shelf.
And just go there to the Y.M.C.A.
I'm sure they can help you today.
*Chorus*

3. Young man, I was once in your shoes.
I said, I was down and out and with the blues.
I felt no man cared if I were alive.
I felt the whole world was so jive.

That's when someone come up to me
And said, "Young man, take a walk up the street.
It's a place there called the Y.M.C.A.
They can start you back on your way."
*Chorus*

# YOU ARE SO BEAUTIFUL

Words and Music by BILLY PRESTON
and BRUCE FISHER

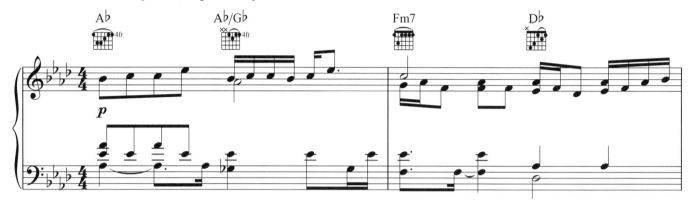

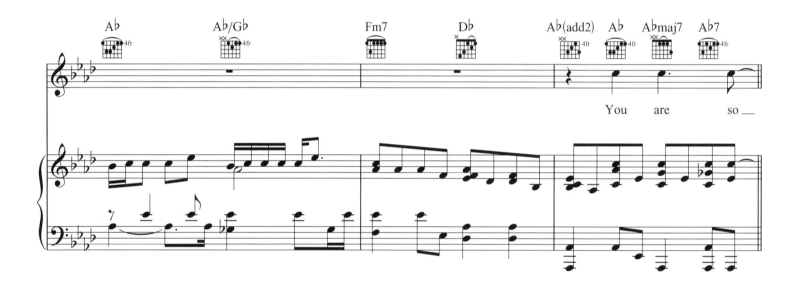

You are so ___

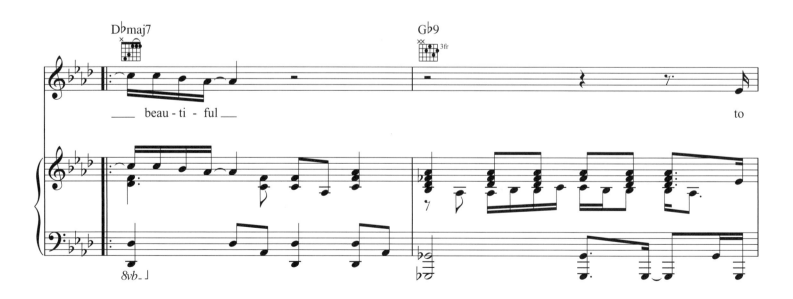

___ beau - ti - ful ___

to

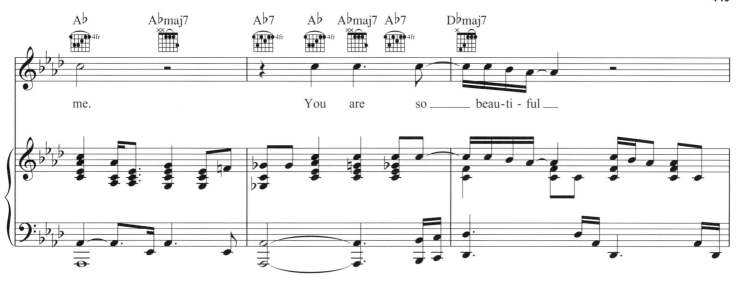

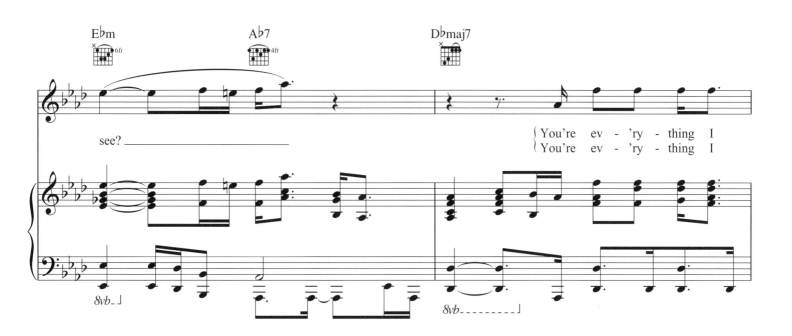

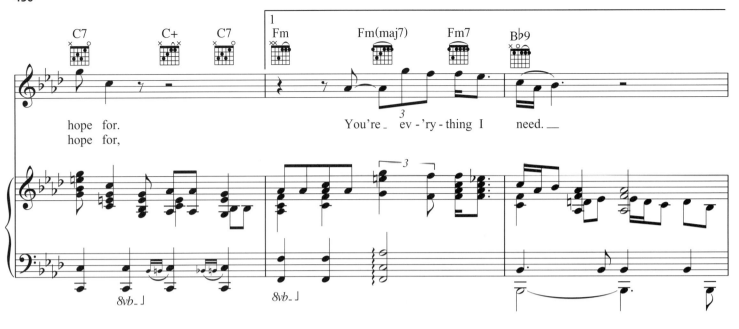

hope for.
hope for,

You're ev-'ry-thing I need.

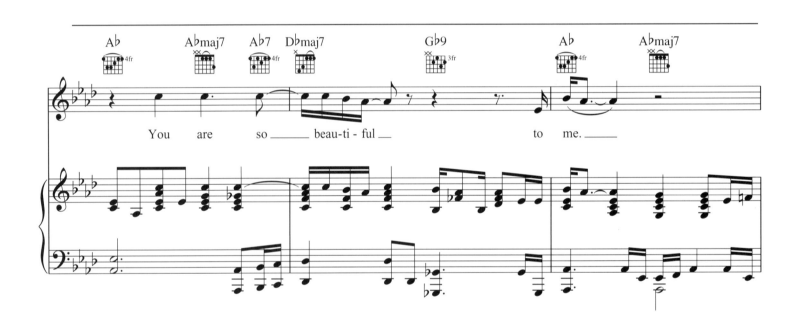

You are so beau-ti-ful to me.

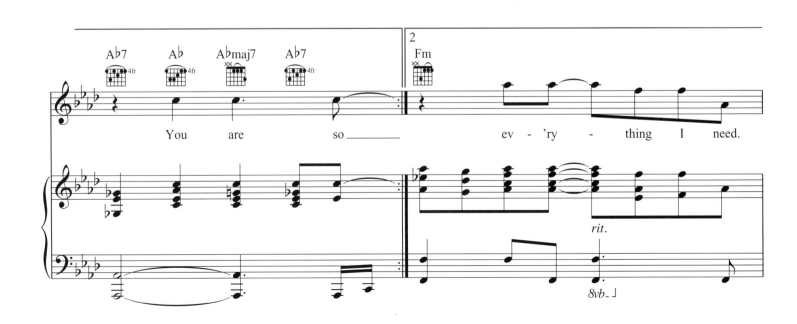

You are so ev-'ry-thing I need.

**Freely**

**Tempo I**

You are so _____ beau - ti - ful \_\_\_\_\_ to \_\_\_\_

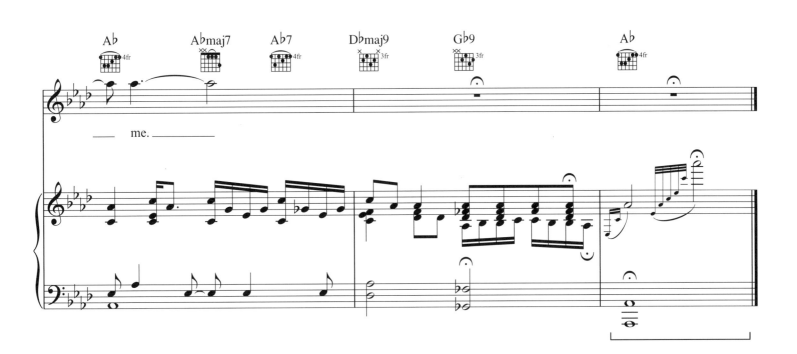

\_\_\_\_ me. _____

# YOU DON'T BRING ME FLOWERS

Words by NEIL DIAMOND,
MARILYN BERGMAN and ALAN BERGMAN
Music by NEIL DIAMOND

**Slowly and freely**

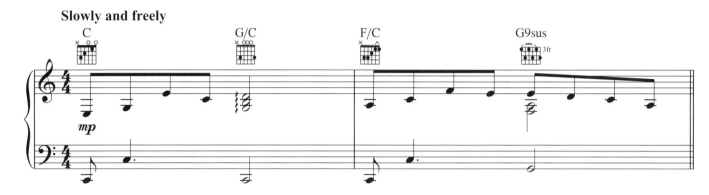

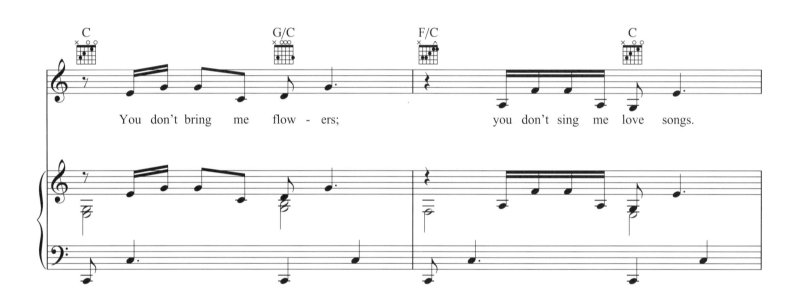

You don't bring me flow - ers; you don't sing me love songs.

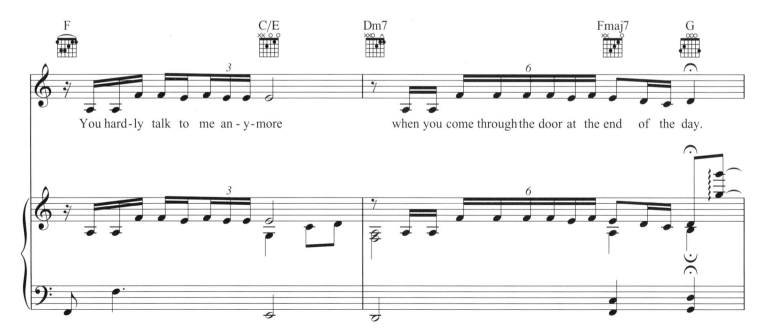

You hard-ly talk to me an-y-more when you come through the door at the end of the day.

# YOU'RE SO VAIN

Words and Music by
CARLY SIMON

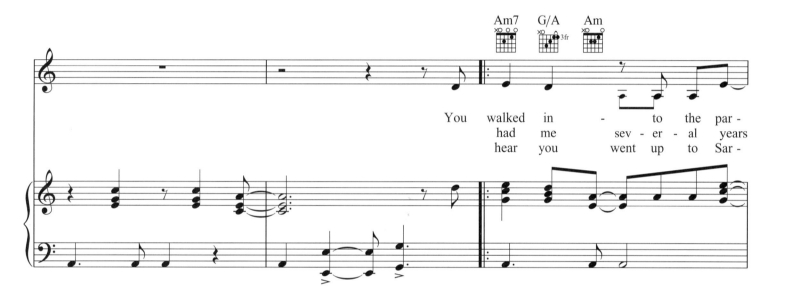

You walked in - to the par -
had me sev - er - al years
hear you went up to Sar -

-ty          like you were    walk - ing on - to ___ a     yacht; ___          your hat stra -
a - go ___          when   I   was still quite ___ na - ive; ___          well, you
a - to - ga, ___          and   your horse nat - 'ral - ly   won; ___          then, you

# YOU'VE GOT A FRIEND

Words and Music by
CAROLE KING

*Cues 2nd time only

# YOUR SONG

Words and Music by ELTON JOHN
and BERNIE TAUPIN

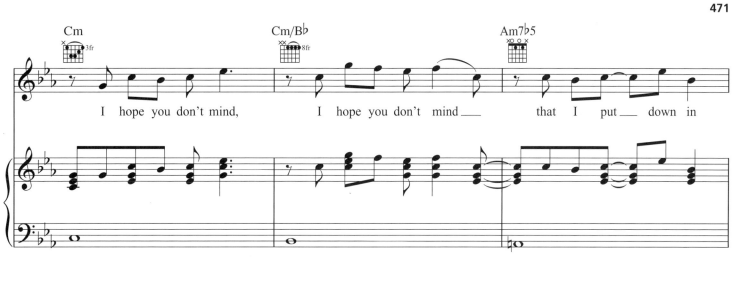

I hope you don't mind, I hope you don't mind ___ that I put ___ down in

words how won - der - ful ___ life is ___ while

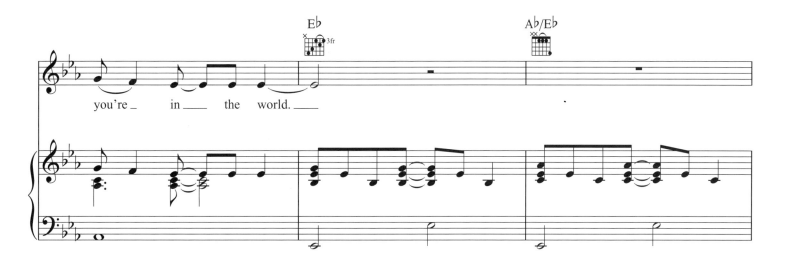

you're _ in ___ the world. ___

*slight rit.*

# THE NEW DECADE SERIES

## Books with Online Audio • Arranged for Piano, Voice, and Guitar

The New Decade Series features collections of iconic songs from each decade with great backing tracks so you can play them and sound like a pro. You access the tracks online for streaming or download. **See complete song listings online at www.halleonard.com**

### SONGS OF THE 1920s

Ain't Misbehavin' • Baby Face • California, Here I Come • Fascinating Rhythm • I Wanna Be Loved by You • It Had to Be You • Mack the Knife • Ol' Man River • Puttin' on the Ritz • Rhapsody in Blue • Someone to Watch over Me • Tea for Two • Who's Sorry Now • and more.
00137576 P/V/G.......................$24.99

### SONGS OF THE 1970s

ABC • Bridge over Troubled Water • Cat's in the Cradle • Dancing Queen • Free Bird • Goodbye Yellow Brick Road • Hotel California • I Will Survive • Joy to the World • Killing Me Softly with His Song • Layla • Let It Be • Piano Man • The Rainbow Connection • Stairway to Heaven • The Way We Were • Your Song • and more.
00137599 P/V/G .......................$27.99

### SONGS OF THE 1930s

As Time Goes By • Blue Moon • Cheek to Cheek • Embraceable You • A Fine Romance • Georgia on My Mind • I Only Have Eyes for You • The Lady Is a Tramp • On the Sunny Side of the Street • Over the Rainbow • Pennies from Heaven • Stormy Weather (Keeps Rainin' All the Time) • The Way You Look Tonight • and more.
00137579 P/V/G.........................$24.99

### SONGS OF THE 1980s

Africa • Beat It • Careless Whisper • Come on Eileen • Don't Stop Believin' • Every Rose Has Its Thorn • Footloose • I Just Called to Say I Love You • Jessie's Girl • Livin' on a Prayer • Saving All My Love for You • Take on Me • Up Where We Belong • The Wind Beneath My Wings • and more.
00137600 P/V/G.......................$27.99

### SONGS OF THE 1940s

At Last • Boogie Woogie Bugle Boy • Don't Get Around Much Anymore • God Bless' the Child • How High the Moon • It Could Happen to You • La Vie En Rose (Take Me to Your Heart Again) • Route 66 • Sentimental Journey • The Trolley Song • You'd Be So Nice to Come Home To • Zip-A-Dee-Doo-Dah • and more.
00137582 P/V/G.......................$24.99

### SONGS OF THE 1990s

Angel • Black Velvet • Can You Feel the Love Tonight • (Everything I Do) I Do It for You • Friends in Low Places • Hero • I Will Always Love You • More Than Words • My Heart Will Go On (Love Theme from 'Titanic') • Smells like Teen Spirit • Under the Bridge • Vision of Love • Wonderwall • and more.
00137601 P/V/G.......................$27.99

### SONGS OF THE 1950s

Ain't That a Shame • Be-Bop-A-Lula • Chantilly Lace • Earth Angel • Fever • Great Balls of Fire • Love Me Tender • Mona Lisa • Peggy Sue • Que Sera, Sera (Whatever Will Be, Will Be) • Rock Around the Clock • Sixteen Tons • A Teenager in Love • That'll Be the Day • Unchained Melody • Volare • You Send Me • Your Cheatin' Heart • and more.
00137595 P/V/G.......................$24.99

### SONGS OF THE 2000s

Bad Day • Beautiful • Before He Cheats • Chasing Cars • Chasing Pavements • Drops of Jupiter (Tell Me) • Fireflies • Hey There Delilah • How to Save a Life • I Gotta Feeling • I'm Yours • Just Dance • Love Story • 100 Years • Rehab • Unwritten • You Raise Me Up • and more.
00137608 P/V/G.......................$27.99

### SONGS OF THE 1960s

All You Need Is Love • Beyond the Sea • Born to Be Wild • California Girls • Dancing in the Street • Happy Together • King of the Road • Leaving on a Jet Plane • Louie, Louie • My Generation • Oh, Pretty Woman • Sunshine of Your Love • Under the Boardwalk • You Really Got Me • and more.
00137596 P/V/G .....................$24.99

## HAL•LEONARD® CORPORATION

7777 W. BLUEMOUND RD. P.O. BOX 13819 MILWAUKEE, WI 53213

**halleonard.com**
Prices, content, and availability subject to change without notice.

1214